DATE DUE

DEMCO INC. 38-2931

CIRCULATING
LIFE

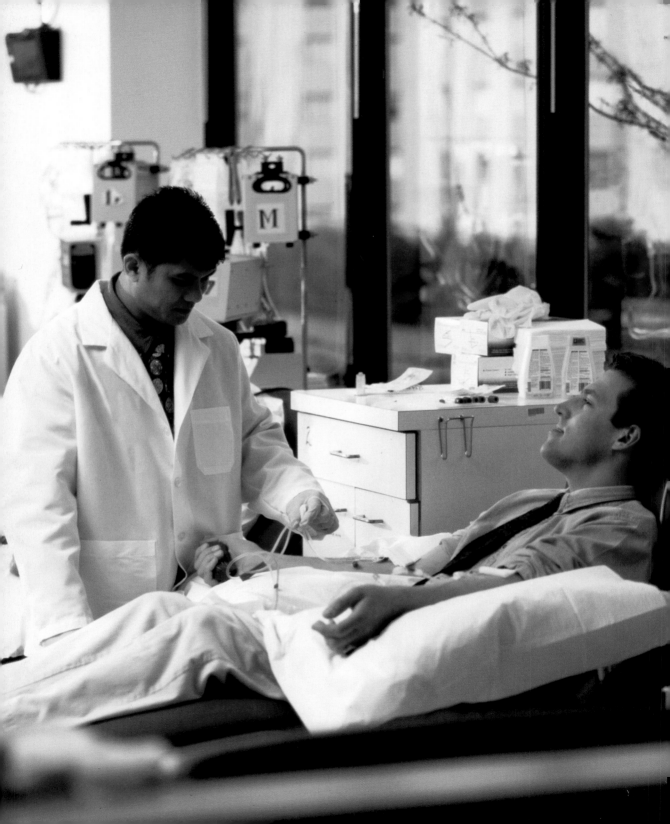

CIRCULATING LIFE

Blood Transfusion from
Ancient Superstition
to Modern Medicine

Cherie Winner

TF
CB Twenty-First Century Books ∎ Minneapolis

To Joelle Riley, gifted editor, science geek, and greyhound mom. You've saved my bacon (and my book) more than once.

Huge thanks to the following for sharing their knowledge of blood and the fascinating field of transfusion medicine: Aaron Long, MD, Ann-Marie Nielson, and Garrett Syphers of St. Mary's Regional Blood Center in Grand Junction CO; Marilyn J. Telen, MD, Wellcome Professor of Medicine at Duke University Medical Cetner, Durham NC; and Ann Schneider, DVM, Director of the Eastern Veterinary Blood Bank, Annapolis MD.

Twenty-First Century Books
A division of Lerner Publishing Group
241 First Avenue North
Minneapolis, MN 55401 U.S.A.

Website address: www.lernerbooks.com

Library of Congress Cataloging-in-Publication Data

Winner, Cherie.
    Circulating life : blood transfusion from ancient superstition to modern medicine / by Cherie Winner.
        p.   cm. — (Discovery!)
    Includes bibliographical references and index.
    ISBN-13: 978–0–8225–6606–9 (lib. bdg. : alk. paper)
    ISBN-10: 0–8225–6606–0 (lib. bdg. : alk. paper)
    1. Blood—Transfusion—Juvenile literature. 2. Blood—Juvenile literature. I. Title.
RM171.W56 2007
615'.39—dc22   2006029921

Manufactured in the United States of America
1 2 3 4 5 6 – BP – 12 11 10 09 08 07

CONTENTS

INTRODUCTION

The pale girl trembles as she hunches over the bowl. She has already thrown up twice. She feels the doctor's gentle hand on her back. The special tea he gave her is beginning to work. A wave of nausea rises inside her, and she tries to throw up again. Not much comes out. The doctor eases her back onto the stacked pillows. "It won't do," he says. "She must be bled." He pulls a delicate knife out of his kit and scrapes it with his thumbnail to remove a crust of blood left over from an earlier patient. The girl's mother hands him the porcelain bowl that had belonged to her great-grandmother. The doctor probes the bend in the girl's arm and makes a quick cut along a vein. "Good," he says, as he watches the dark fluid stream out into the bowl.

This doctor is not a quack. He is a skilled physician in the year 1592. Christopher Columbus reached the New World a century ago. Here in London, England, the Old World is buzzing with new discoveries in physics, navigation, and medicine. The doctor takes pride in following the latest developments, but he also knows that sometimes the old ways are best. He is certain he is doing the right thing for his young patient. After all, doctors had been bleeding their patients for more than two thousand years.

Flash forward to a present-day emergency room (ER), gleaming with polished floors and sterilized instruments. A

This drawing from the late 1500s shows a physician bleeding a patient.

man is rushed in from the scene of a car accident. He doesn't have major wounds, but he is unconscious and pale, with a fast, weak pulse and very low blood pressure. All signs point to massive internal bleeding. The doctor orders a transfusion of red blood cells. Once the cells are in the man's veins, they will carry oxygen to his tissues. They will keep him alive until surgeons can repair his injuries.

Transfusion—putting blood or blood products into a person—is one of the first treatments the ER doctor thinks of. She trusts the blood bank to provide this "gift of life" as soon as she places the call. For her, putting blood into a patient is as natural as taking blood out was for her predecessor.

Transfusion saves thousands of lives every year. Yet blood can still surprise us with its ability to cause harm. Transfusions done to restore health sometimes kill, by spreading new diseases such as acquired immunodeficiency syndrome (AIDS).

Over the centuries, our ideas about blood have changed. But blood still plays a central role in human medicine, both for good and bad and for life and death.

Chapter 1

A FINE HUMOR—
EARLY IDEAS ABOUT BLOOD

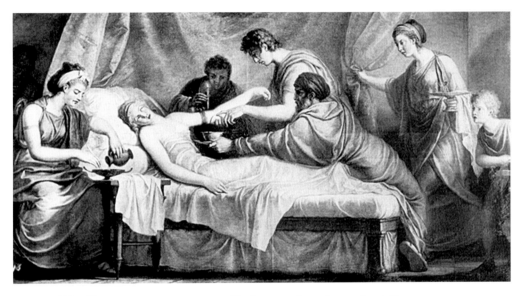

Bleeding was a common medical procedure in ancient Greece.

Bleeding a person who is already sick sounds barbaric. Until the 1800s, however, it was one of the most common medical treatments in the world. Almost every culture, in every era, has used it.

In prehistoric times, people believed that demons in the body caused illness. To heal a sick person, the demons had to be removed. Healers cast magic spells to drive some demons away. Other demons were believed to live in the blood. These could be expelled only by bleeding the patient. Shamans poked their patients with a thorn, a fish tooth, or a sharp rock to get blood to flow.

(9)

The great thinkers of ancient Greece (about 600 to 300 B.C.) also thought bleeding could cure many illnesses. They believed that health requires a balance of four humors. That doesn't mean telling an equal number of limericks, riddles, knock-knock jokes, and puns. In this case, the word *humor* means "fluid." The ancient Greeks believed that four bodily fluids—blood, yellow bile, black bile, and phlegm—determined a person's physical and mental health. When the four humors were in balance, the person was healthy and rational. If there was too much of one compared to the others, the person became ill or insane. The cure for any illness was to remove some of the excess humor.

Each of the four humors was thought to correspond to a different personality type. In this astrological chart from Germany in the fifteenth century, the types are labeled "flegmat" (phlegmatic, caused by excess phlegm), "sangvin" (sanguine, caused by excess blood), "maelanc" (melancholy, caused by excess black bile), and "coleric" (choleric, caused by excess yellow bile).

An upset stomach indicated too much yellow bile. The body's natural way of getting rid of excess yellow bile was to vomit. The doctor would give a drug called an emetic to make the patient vomit more. Constipation or lack of energy meant the patient had too much black bile. A strong laxative would empty the bowels. Chest congestion resulted from too much phlegm. Various remedies helped the body get rid of the surplus, much as we use cough syrups today.

Doctors thought excess blood or too much heat in the blood caused many symptoms. If a patient had a fever, headache, swelling, or pain, the doctor would probably prescribe reducing the amount of blood. Even broken bones were treated by bleeding the patient.

After any treatment, the physician waited for a few hours to see how the patient responded. If the patient remained ill, the humors must still be out of balance. Further action was needed. Usually, this meant more bleeding. The doctor could always get a little more blood out of a patient. People were often bled two or more times a day. They lost several ounces of blood each time, until they recovered—or died.

A Passion for Bleeding

Over the centuries, bleeding became the most common medical treatment. Books were written about it. Diagrams showed where the patient should be cut to cure different ailments. Astrological charts, which were used to predict the future based on the positions of the Sun, Moon, planets, and stars, showed the luckiest times of the month to bleed patients.

Surgeons invented special techniques for bleeding. In a treatment called cupping, the doctor heated a glass bulb and then

Tractatabus de Pestilentia (Treatise on Plague), *written in eastern Europe in the 1400s, includes this woodcut showing patients being cupped.*

placed its open end on the patient's bare skin. As the glass cooled, a vacuum formed inside the bulb and pulled on the flesh to create a blister of blood. The doctor then removed the bulb and opened the blister with a scarificator, a small box bearing up to a dozen rotating blades. When the doctor slid the box over the blister, the turning blades sliced the skin, releasing the pooled blood. Another popular technique was to place bloodsucking leeches on the skin and let them feed for several minutes. We have since learned that losing a lot of blood over a period of days or weeks will probably make us sick. It certainly won't help us get better. But back then, doctors didn't keep careful records of what worked, what didn't work, and what needed further testing. When a patient recovered after being bled, the success was attributed to the bleeding. When a patient died, doctors thought the bleeding had been done too late or the illness was just too strong to be defeated.

Although bleeding was very common, the opposite idea—putting more blood into a patient—didn't occur to early doctors. The Greeks sometimes drank the blood of a fallen warrior to gain his courage and strength. They believed the blood they drank would be converted into their own blood in their liver. But transfusion probably wouldn't have made sense to them. Blood was the most special of the four humors. It was believed to carry the very essence of the person, including the person's genetic inheritance. That's where we get the term *bloodline*. The Greeks believed that the honor of fathers passed to their sons through the blood. Putting blood from one person directly into another person's bloodstream might have seemed to them a violation, a pollution of the individual self.

Tradition Rules

Greek ideas about medicine dominated Europe for almost two thousand years. The bridge between the Greeks and later Europeans was a doctor named Galen. During the second century A.D., Galen practiced medicine in Rome.

Like other Greek doctors, Galen had never dissected a human body. It was illegal to cut open a corpse to study it. He learned anatomy, the structure and arrangement of parts of the body, by looking at people from the outside, by dissecting animals, and by treating the wounds of gladiators and soldiers.

Despite his lack of anatomical knowledge, Galen was a gifted healer for his time. He became the official doctor to Rome's leading families, and he wrote books that carefully spelled out the theory of the four humors. One of his favorite treatments was bleeding.

In his books, Galen said that when we breathe in, a spiritual substance called pneuma enters the heart and makes it beat. He said the blood in veins is dark because it carries nutrients from the stomach and liver and that the blood in arteries is bright red because it carries pneuma from the heart. He thought both kinds of blood move away from the heart in an endless red tide washing outward through the body.

Galen became the world's foremost authority on medicine. Long after he died, other doctors turned to his work for answers, rather than searching for solutions themselves.

If a medical student ever doubted what he read in Galen's books, he had no way to test his ideas. Medical schools didn't even teach anatomy. The laws forbidding dissection were finally

Galen (A.D. 129–200), one of the most famous physicians in the ancient world, influenced the practice of medicine for hundreds of years.

changed in the 1300s, but students still weren't allowed to work with corpses themselves. Instead, a teaching assistant did the dissection while a professor read from one of Galen's books. Students watched and listened. If what they saw in the corpse did not match what Galen said, the corpse was wrong. Students who dared to disagree with Galen's ideas were kicked out of school. Teachers who disagreed lost their jobs and had their homes ransacked. Some were even executed.

After graduation, the new doctors still didn't do much hands-on work. Doctors only diagnosed illnesses and prescribed treatments. In modern times, surgeons are the highest-paid, highest-status doctors. But back then, bleeding, bone setting, and most kinds of surgery were considered to be manual labor and beneath a physician's dignity. These tasks were done by surgeons, who learned their trade from practicing surgeons rather than through university education. Surgery wasn't even a full-time job for most surgeons. Bloodletting was a "side business" for many barbers.

Over time, anatomy and dissection finally became a standard part of medical education. Surgical skills gained more respect as medical education began to include more hands-on work, such as anatomical dissection. Physicians began to bleed patients themselves.

The Great Breakthrough

Starting in the 1300s, change began to sweep through Europe. Artists such as Michelangelo and Leonardo da Vinci studied anatomy so their paintings and sculptures would be more true to life. Scientists began looking for new evidence to support their ideas rather than simply accepting the authority of ancient books. As they studied the human body, they compared what they found with what Galen had written. They found that Galen had often been wrong.

Curious investigators found that some blood vessels contained valves that prevented blood from flowing away from the heart. To these people, the system of arteries and veins looked like a loop. These new observations didn't fit Galen's description of blood flowing continuously outward from the heart.

Figuring out how a living body works by studying corpses is nearly impossible. In the late 1500s and early 1600s, scientists began to conduct experiments to find out what was really going on. These scientists studied living people and animals. They made changes in a living body and watched how the body functioned after the change.

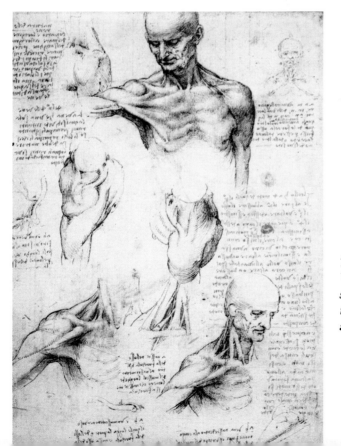

The artist Leonardo da Vinci (1452–1519) spent a great deal of time studying human anatomy.

THE CIRCULATORY SYSTEM

The body's blood vessels form two separate loops, with the heart at the crossover point. In each loop, arteries carry blood away from the heart and veins carry blood toward the heart.

The systemic loop carries oxygen-rich blood to all the tissues of the body. In the capillaries, the blood delivers oxygen to the body's cells and picks up carbon dioxide produced by the cells. The oxygen-poor blood then returns to the heart, which sends it through the pulmonary loop to the lungs. There, the blood exchanges its load of carbon dioxide for oxygen. Then it returns to the heart as bright red, oxygen-rich blood ready to be sent out in the systemic loop again.

Arteries and veins are largest near the heart. They branch and become smaller the farther they are from the heart. Blood flows from the tiniest arteries to the tiniest veins through capillaries, which are so narrow that blood cells pass through them in single file. Over all, a human body contains about 60,000 miles (100,000 kilometers) of blood vessels.

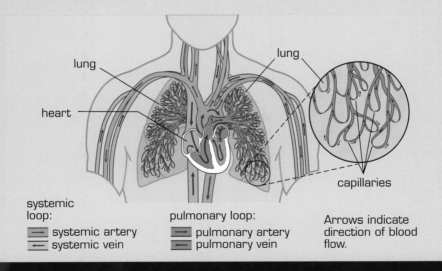

systemic loop:
→ systemic artery
← systemic vein

pulmonary loop:
→ pulmonary artery
← pulmonary vein

Arrows indicate direction of blood flow.

Italian physician Andrea Cesalpino used a ligature, or constricting band, like a tourniquet. He tied a string around a dog's blood vessel, tightly enough to stop the flow of blood. The ligature acted like a dam across a river. "Downstream" from the ligature, the vessel emptied as the blood within it flowed on through the system. "Upstream," the vessel swelled as it filled with more and more blood. When he loosened the ligature, the dammed-up blood rushed on through the vessel. Using this technique, Cesalpino showed that veins carry blood toward the heart, not away from it as Galen had said.

In two books published in the late 1500s, Cesalpino described the human circulatory system. He said it was a loop in which arteries carry blood away from the heart and veins bring it back toward the heart. He realized that in order to complete the loop, blood must somehow get from very small arteries to very small veins. He suggested that arteries and veins were connected by tiny vessels he called capillaries. That was just a guess. He couldn't actually see capillaries, because microscopes hadn't been invented yet.

A Key Calculation

Not everyone was convinced by Cesalpino's work. Many physicians were unwilling to admit that Galen had been so wrong about something so basic. They needed more proof. A few decades later, British physician William Harvey gave it to them.

Harvey came up with new ways of thinking about the body. He used measurements and math to answer questions about how the body works. He also looked at the heart and blood vessels as a mechanical system, like an arrangement of pipes carrying fluid driven by a pump. No one had ever looked at the human body in that way before.

It's almost impossible to watch a mammal's heart in action and see what it's doing. It moves too fast. Harvey realized that the hearts of cold-blooded animals beat more slowly. He spent many hours watching a living snake's heart push blood through its body.

Once Harvey realized that the heart works as a pump, he wondered how much blood it moves in a given amount of time. He knew from autopsies that an adult human's heart holds about 2 ounces (60 milliliters) of blood. He estimated that about 0.5 ounce (15 ml) was pumped out with every heart beat. Multiplying that amount by the average number of beats per half hour, Harvey figured the heart moves as much as 375 gallons (1,420 liters) of blood weighing nearly 4,000 pounds (1,800 kilograms) every day!

Harvey's work showed that instead of a steady flow of new blood, the body must contain a small amount of blood that circulates back through the heart many times every day. Doctors have since learned that the average adult man has within him 5 to 6 quarts (4.7 to 5.7 l) of blood weighing 10 to 12 pounds (4.5 to 5.4 kg). The blood makes a complete loop through his body about fifty times every hour.

Harvey did other experiments showing that blood circulates. He didn't get everything right, though. He thought blood passed from arteries to veins through tiny pores in the tissue rather than through capillaries. But he conducted such beautiful, clear experiments that his 1628 book, *On the Motion of the Heart and Blood in Animals*, is usually named as the first written proof that blood circulates.

After Harvey's work, people thought of blood as a substance that scientists could measure and manipulate and whose path in the body could be traced. Yet medical practice didn't change right away. Bleeding remained as popular as ever. Harvey himself called for a surgeon to bleed him whenever he became ill.

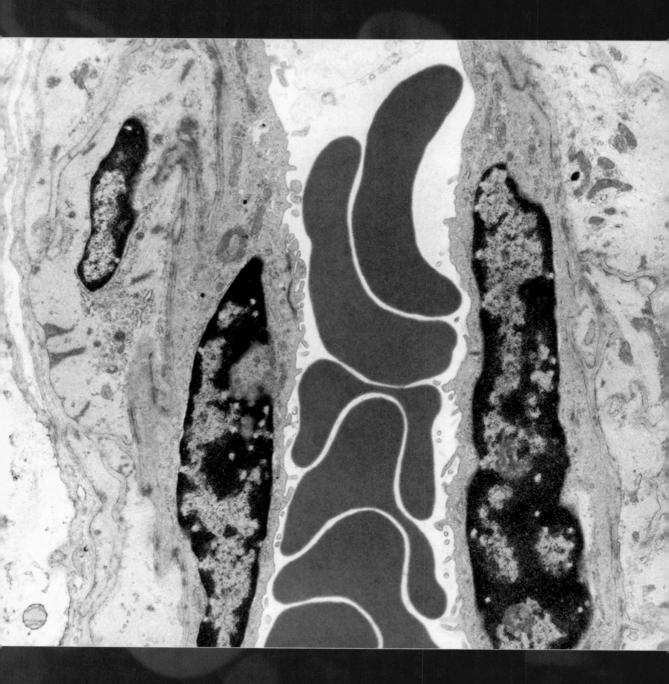

Chapter 2

A CLOSER LOOK AT BLOOD

Early scientists knew that blood was essential for life, but they had no idea how complex blood is and how many jobs it does in the body. We now know that blood carries oxygen from the lungs to every cell in the body and carries carbon dioxide from the cells to the lungs. It distributes hormones, chemicals that are made in one part of the body and affect target tissues elsewhere in the body. It carries nutrients from the digestive system to all the cells of the body and wastes from the cells to the kidneys. It provides all tissues of the body with the water they need. It fights infection. It detects and tries to destroy invaders. And it repairs small holes in blood vessels and forms clots to reduce bleeding. To do all these jobs, blood has many parts, including different kinds of cells and hundreds of chemicals.

In just 34 millionths of an ounce (1 microliter) of your blood are 4 to 6 million red blood cells, 4,000 to 12,000 white blood cells, and 150,000 to 400,000 platelets (fragments of cells). Together, the cells and platelets are called formed elements.

Red Blood Cells

A red blood cell looks like a round pillow with a dimple in each side. Like a pillow, a red blood cell is flexible. It can change its shape to squeeze through narrow capillaries. Red blood cells are also called RBCs, or erythrocytes.

Red blood cells are squeezed together as they pass through a tiny blood vessel as shown in this micrograph.

Each erythrocyte is stuffed full of hemoglobin, a protein that can carry both oxygen and carbon dioxide. All of the cells in your body depend on the hemoglobin in RBCs to bring them the oxygen they need and to remove the carbon dioxide they produce during metabolism, the chemical processes all living cells perform.

The surface of a red blood cell is covered with proteins and glycoproteins, which are proteins with sugars attached to them. The specific sugars your red blood cells carry determine what blood type you have—A, B, AB, or O.

Most red blood cells live for a few months at most. Then they die and fall apart. Your body continuously makes new red blood cells to replace those being lost.

Problems with red blood cells cause a variety of conditions known as anemia. A person who has too few red blood cells or too little hemoglobin is said to be anemic. Some people, especially people of African descent, have a hereditary disease called sickle-cell anemia. This disease causes the body to produce abnormal hemoglobin. It doesn't carry as much oxygen as it should, and it makes the RBCs become curved, or sickle shaped. Sickle-shaped RBCs may damage capillaries.

Normal red blood cells are shaped like round pillows. Sickle-cell anemia changes the shape of some of the RBCs.

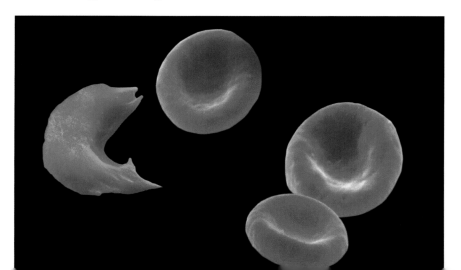

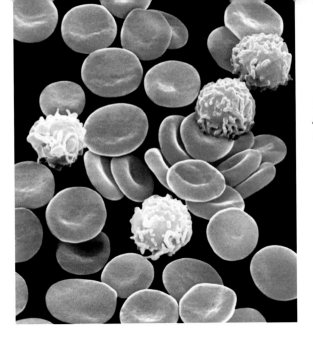

White blood cells are spherical, with a bumpy surface.

White Blood Cells

White blood cells are also called leukocytes. Our blood contains five kinds of leukocytes: neutrophils, basophils, lymphocytes, eosinophils, and monocytes. Each does a specific job. Neutrophils attack bacteria directly. They are the first line of defense against bacterial infection. Basophils produce chemicals that help protect the body against invaders. Some of these chemicals, such as histamine, cause symptoms we recognize as an allergic reaction. Lymphocytes produce antibodies, which are proteins that recognize and attack foreign material such as bacteria and viruses. The pus in a pimple is made of millions of white cells that converged to attack bacteria that infected the body at that point. The function of eosinophils isn't well understood, but they produce toxic chemicals that may kill infectious cells. Monocytes gobble up the debris that remains after the other leukocytes have killed the invading cells.

Together, the leukocytes battle infection and act as the bloodstream's "garbage crew." They usually leave the blood vessels and enter other tissues to do their work. For them, blood vessels are simply a rapid-transit system that gets them where they need to go. Some white blood cells live just a few months. Others, such as lymphocytes, may last your whole life.

Any problem with leukocytes can cause serious illness. A person with too few leukocytes has a hard time fighting off infections. Having too many leukocytes can be even worse than having too few. The disease called leukemia develops when a person's system makes far too many leukocytes. The extra white cells damage the kidneys, brain, and liver. Other problems arise when the white cells come under attack from bacteria or viruses. Lymphocytes called T cells are the main targets of human immunodeficiency virus (HIV), the virus that causes AIDS. When T cells become infected with HIV, they lose the ability to fight off other infections.

Platelets

Platelets are also known as thrombocytes. They look like tiny cells, but they are actually just cell fragments. They form when bits of cytoplasm, the living matter of a cell, pinch off from megakaryocytes, huge cells found in bone marrow (the spongy tissue inside bones). Platelets live for only seven to ten days.

Platelets do two crucial jobs. First, they plug small holes that form in blood vessel walls, until the blood vessel itself can do a more permanent repair job. Second, if a blood vessel is more badly damaged, platelets help stop the bleeding. They kick off a series of chemical reactions known as the clotting cascade. At the end of the cascade, a clot forms. The clot blocks further loss of blood. Clots also form when blood is exposed to air. If you cut yourself, blood will clot at the site of injury. The clot will eventually develop into a scab.

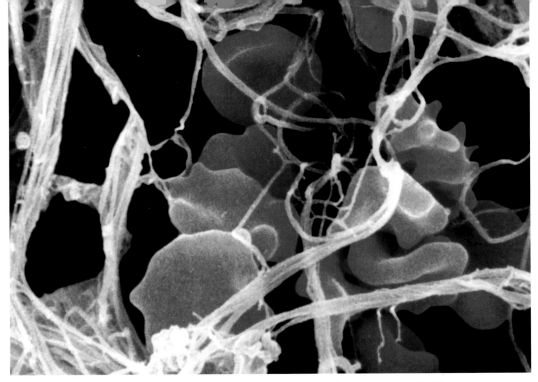

A blood clot is a three-dimensional mesh of platelets, protein fibers, and red blood cells.

The clotting cascade must be carefully balanced. Blood that clots too easily can cause a heart attack or stroke by blocking the flow of blood to parts of the body. Blood that doesn't clot well enough can cause a person to bleed to death from a minor wound.

Some clotting problems, such as thrombocytopenia, result from having too few platelets. People with von Willebrand's disease have the right number of platelets, but they don't work right. The best-known disease caused by failure to clot is hemophilia. People with hemophilia have normal platelets, but they lack clotting factors, substances that play necessary roles in the clotting cascade. Three forms of hemophilia exist. Each is caused by a different inherited mutation that results in the person not having a necessary clotting factor. All the clotting factors are dissolved in the liquid part of the blood, which is called plasma.

Plasma

Blood is about half liquid. If you let a blood sample stand for several minutes, it will separate into three distinct layers. At the bottom, taking up 40 to 50 percent of the volume, is a dark red layer of red blood cells. Above that is a thin, yellow white layer called the buffy coat, which contains white blood cells and platelets. The top 50 to 60 percent of the sample is the yellowish or pinkish, clear plasma.

Plasma is mostly water, with many materials dissolved in it. It contains salts such as sodium chloride and calcium carbonate; wastes such as uric acid; nutrients such as glucose, amino acids, and fats; and hormones such as adrenaline. Some of the most important substances in plasma are proteins.

Clotting factors and fibrinogen are proteins that team up with platelets and calcium to form clots. The clotting substances flow through the body all the time. Damage to a blood

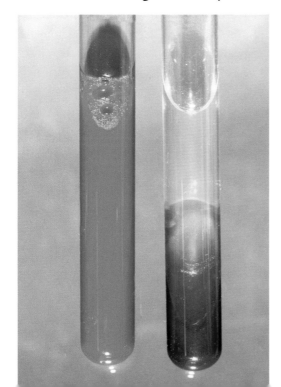

The test tube on the left contains whole blood. In the test tube on the right, the RBCs have settled to the bottom, leaving a layer of plasma at the top.

vessel activates them. As platelets are making a plug at the site of the injury, clotting factors change fibrinogen into a long, stringy protein called fibrin. Many strands of fibrin weave together with the platelets and RBCs to form a clot. Other proteins in the plasma keep the clot from getting too big. After the injury heals, they dissolve the clot.

You can see the clotting process at work in a single drop of blood. The color changes from bright red to dark red as oxygen leaves the hemoglobin. After several minutes, the blood separates into two distinct parts: the fibrous clot, which is dark red, and a clear, pinkish fluid called serum. Blood serum is what is left of plasma after the clotting factors have been removed or used up.

Antibodies are proteins in the blood that recognize and attack foreign substances such as bacteria. Some antibodies, such as those that recognize blood cells from a person with a different blood type, are in the blood all the time. Others, such as those that recognize infectious agents, show up only after the body is exposed to the foreign substance.

The most abundant protein in plasma is albumin. It helps maintain a healthy blood pressure by keeping water in the blood vessels. High blood pressure can cause kidney failure, heart attack, or stroke. Low blood pressure can prevent cells throughout the body from receiving the oxygen and nutrients they need.

None of the components of blood were known in Harvey's day. He and the scientists who followed him in the 1600s knew nothing about blood types, what causes clotting, or even that there are such things as cells. When they began to do transfusions, they still thought of blood as a humor that influenced a person's character as well as his health.

Chapter 3

THE FIRST TRANSFUSIONS

The experiments of Cesalpino and Harvey inspired scientists throughout Europe to continue investigating the world around them. In England in the seventeenth century, top thinkers in all fields gathered to form a group called the Royal Society. Doctors, chemists, botanists, astronomers, architects, and other professionals were welcome. At their monthly meetings, members showed off their latest experiments and debated what the results meant. It was an exciting time, ripe with new ideas and the chance to make great discoveries.

Similar groups formed in other countries. Each country's scientists wanted to be the first to succeed with a new experiment or treatment. The English and the French especially tried to outdo each other.

Infusion Experiments

One hot area of research built on the discovery of circulation. Scientists reasoned that if blood circulates, it should be able to carry materials all throughout the body. In the 1650s and 1660s, they tested this idea by infusing (injecting) substances into a dog's leg vein and watching to see what happened.

Experimenters used syringes made of the hollow quill of a feather. They sharpened one end of the quill and slipped a small

The Royal Society of London for Improving Natural Knowledge was founded in 1660.

bladder, or balloonlike sac, over the other end, like the bulb on a turkey baster. When they squeezed the bladder, it forced whatever was in the quill out the sharp end.

The first substance they infused was opium, a powerful narcotic drug. It quickly made the dog sleepy and disoriented. This experiment was a great success, since it showed that the dog's bloodstream carried the drug from the leg to the brain.

Many other infusion experiments followed. Researchers tried infusing alcohol, medications, and acids. Some of the dogs recovered to live out their days as honored pets. Many others did not survive their ordeal.

Soon the scientists tried infusing human subjects. They were much more cautious about what they infused into people, however. All their human subjects survived.

A young English doctor named Richard Lower became an infusion expert. Lower thought he might be able to nourish a patient who was too sick to eat by injecting nutrients into the patient's bloodstream. He tried infusing dogs with broth or milk. The results were disappointing. The dogs usually died. Lower autopsied them and found their blood curdled in the vessels. He concluded that milk and broth were too different from blood to mix with it. He needed to find a substance that was more like blood. Why not use blood itself?

Early Transfusions

Lower first tried transfusion in 1665. Working with dogs, he set up the experiment so blood flowed directly from the donor into the recipient. The two animals were tied down side by side. Lower cut away the tissue that covered a blood vessel of each animal. (Doctors hadn't yet figured out that they could reach a blood vessel through the skin.) He inserted dried reeds or silver tubes into the blood vessels. He connected the two tubes with a length of artery from a cow. After several false starts, Lower found that the best arrangement connected the donor's artery to the recipient's vein. Arterial blood, propelled by the donor's heart, surged through the tubes and into the recipient.

Lower's experiments were often messy. Blood spattered everywhere. They were also dirty in a medical way: the materials were not sterilized. Lower didn't know that microbes—germs—even existed. Every time he cut open an animal or inserted a quill into a blood vessel, he exposed the creature to millions of bacteria.

Lower removed some of the recipient's blood before doing the experiment, to make room for the new blood that would be coming in. He measured how much he removed by draining it into a bowl or cup. Measuring how much blood went in during the transfusion wasn't so easy. In fact, it was impossible. Lower estimated the amount by watching the clock. He let the transfusion go on for as long as he thought it would take for the right amount of blood to pass.

In February 1666, Lower did a dramatic experiment. He drained so much blood from the recipient that the dog passed out. Then he hooked up a donor dog and let its blood flow into the unconscious one. Within a few minutes, the recipient revived! Lower repeated the procedure, draining out enough blood to make the dog faint again and then transfusing it with blood from a second donor. Again, the dog revived. After having his wound stitched up and his restraints loosened, the dog jumped off the table, shook himself, and went outside to play.

Lower didn't publish a report on his transfusions right away. He wanted to do more experiments and be more sure of the results before spreading the news. But he also wanted the credit that was due him for being first. In December 1666, he published a paper on his work with dogs. The paper staked his claim as the first to do a successful transfusion. It also told other scientists how he had done it. Once his techniques were published, anyone could read and learn from them.

Lower's experiment amazed the scientific community. Blood from one animal had brought another animal back from the brink of death! Members of the Royal Society speculated about possible uses for transfusion. One colleague sent Lower a list of sixteen questions he thought transfusion experiments would answer. They included:

- If blood from a timid dog is transfused into a fierce dog, will the fierce dog become tamer?
- Will a dog that knows how to fetch lose that training after getting blood from a dog that lacks the skill?
- Does transfusion change the recipient's size or hair color

Lower and other transfusionists did experiments to try to answer some of these questions. Although they usually used dogs, they also transfused blood from a steer into a lamb (the lamb lived), from a dog into a sheep (the sheep's death three days later was blamed on a prior illness), and from a lamb into a fox (the fox died a day later). But before Lower and others could fully explore transfusion between different kinds of animals, their competitive spirit swept them into experiments with human beings.

Transfusing Humans

The rush was on. All over Europe, scientists started trying transfusions. Since Lower had already done it with animals, the obvious next step was to transfuse blood into a person.

Lower hesitated. He knew the recipients of transfusion often died, and he didn't want to risk the life of a human being. Furthermore, transfusion might be a bad thing even if the patient lived. If transfusion changed a person's character, wasn't that tinkering with God's creation? Would it be immoral to put an animal's blood into a human being?

While Lower held back, a young doctor in France boldly took the next step. Jean-Baptiste Denis was a first-rate surgeon. Like Lower, he belonged to a scientific society whose members made eager audiences for his demonstrations.

Denis had little practice with transfusion. He didn't even try transfusing dogs until after reading Lower's paper. His early attempts were messy failures. He kept working at it, though, and quickly improved. He even came up with an important advance: he inserted the tube into a blood vessel through the skin, rather than cutting open the animal to expose the vessel. That spared the animal a lot of pain and probably reduced the risk of infection.

In June 1667, three months after his first attempt to transfuse a dog, Denis performed the first ever transfusion into a human being. The recipient was a boy of fifteen or sixteen years old who had been ill with a fever for two months.

Most earlier transfusions had involved transfers between members of the same species (dogs). But when it came to transfusing humans, doctors generally agreed that the donor should not be another person. They doubted that anyone would voluntarily give up some of his own blood. Besides, they considered animals' blood to be more pure. All human blood was thought to be tainted by immoral behavior, powerful emotions, or poor eating and drinking habits. Putting blood from one person into another might transfer all that was bad about the donor to the recipient. Blood from animals, especially mild-mannered ones such as lambs and calves, was expected to dilute the recipient's bad blood, restoring a sense of order to even the sickest human being. So Denis chose a lamb to donate blood for the first human transfusion.

The recipient, whose name was not recorded, had received standard medical care during his illness. He had been bled twenty times, or about once every three days. When Denis met him, the boy still had a fever. He was also weak and not very sharp mentally. He slept a lot. He was probably severely anemic.

Denis agreed with bleeding as a treatment in many cases, but he thought that this boy had been bled too much. He thought adding more blood might dilute the fever and restore the boy's health.

Early on the morning of June 15, 1667, Denis and his assistant slit a vein in the boy's arm—the same one we use today for drawing blood—and let out 3 ounces (90 ml) of blood. (Since the boy had already been bled so much, it's not clear why they did this.) Then they inserted a tube into the carotid artery in the lamb's neck and connected it to the tube in the boy's vein.

Almost immediately, the boy said his arm felt hot. Denis counted off the minutes. When he guessed about 9 ounces (270 ml) of blood had been transferred, he removed the tubes and bound up the wounds. Then he waited and watched.

A few hours later, the boy perked up. He stayed awake for hours, and he ate lunch. Those were good signs. He also had a small nosebleed, which did not alarm Lower. A modern doctor, however, would have recognized it as a sign that the boy's system was reacting against the foreign blood. Later, he slept briefly. From the next day on, he felt much better. His fever disappeared, and he felt lively again. He went to work for Denis as a valet.

It was a promising result, but one that puzzles modern doctors. The nosebleed and the heat in the boy's arm indicate his body was reacting against the foreign blood. The reaction was mild, so perhaps the boy didn't receive enough of the lamb's blood to make him sicker. But that wouldn't explain why he got better. Some have suggested he improved because he wasn't being bled anymore and his system had a chance to rebuild itself. But that process would have taken weeks, and the boy felt better within two days of the transfusion. His recovery remains a medical mystery.

Competition

In England, the members of the Royal Society were furious at the news of Denis's experiment. In their official journal, they hinted that Denis had been reckless in rushing ahead with human transfusion. They claimed that English scientists would have transfused into a person long ago if they hadn't been worried about the danger to the recipient.

Lower was still concerned about the risks, but he wasn't about to let Denis have all the glory. He prepared to do the experiment himself. He wanted a subject who was physically healthy but not quite right mentally. He feared that if a physically sick man received a transfusion and then died, there would be no way of knowing whether the illness or the transfusion had killed him. Mental illness was different. If a madman's physical condition changed after he received a transfusion, Lower would know the new blood was responsible.

Lower found his perfect subject in Arthur Coga, a thirty-two-year-old former pastor who was mildly depressed. The transfusion was performed on November 23, 1667. Blood ran from a

In 1667 Richard Lower transfused blood from a sheep into a man.

sheep's carotid artery into the vein in Coga's arm for about one minute. Coga did not mention feeling heat in his arm. Over the next several days, he felt calmer than he had in a long time. He asked Lower to do the procedure again. On December 14, Lower transfused Coga a second time. Again, all went well.

But that was the last human transfusion that would be done in England for 150 years. Across the English Channel in France, Denis was discovering the very real dangers of transfusion.

An Experiment Goes Wrong

Denis didn't rest on his early success. For his next experiment, he found a subject much like Lower's—a physically healthy man with mental problems. Antoine Mauroy, forty-five, was a laborer who went through spells in which he picked fights in bars and beat up his wife. Denis chose a calf as donor in hopes that its calm demeanor would cool the madness in Mauroy's blood.

On December 18, 1667, Denis drained 10 ounces (300 ml) of blood from Mauroy's arm. He hooked up a series of tubes from Mauroy's vein to an artery on the calf's inner thigh. The spectators—members of Denis's scientific society—crowded in so closely that Denis got pushed aside. By the time he wedged his way back to Mauroy, the blood had clotted in the tubes. When Denis separated the tubes to clear them, blood from the calf's pulsing artery sprayed the room.

Finally, Denis got everything working right. As the blood flowed, Mauroy complained of heat in his arm. He started to faint. Denis ended the procedure. He had transfused very little blood.

The next morning, Mauroy was quiet. It seemed like a change for the better. Denis prepared to do a second transfusion, just two days after the first. This time, an even larger crowd attended. They had heard about the exciting events of the previous demonstration and wanted to see the spectacle for themselves.

This time, the procedure went smoothly. Denis managed to transfuse a large amount of blood. Mauroy again complained of heat in his arm. Then his pulse and temperature shot up. His lower back hurt, his stomach ached, and he felt like he was choking. For nearly two hours, he vomited and had diarrhea. He produced large amounts of black urine. Finally, the symptoms eased, and he was able to sleep.

Modern doctors recognize that Mauroy's system was reacting against the foreign blood. As violent as the reaction was, though, he woke up the next morning much calmer than he was before. His wife reported that over the next few days he treated her better.

Denis agreed that Mauroy looked better, but he saw hints that all was not well. Mauroy still felt pain in his stomach. He was weak, he had a terrible nosebleed, and he continued to produce black urine. Soon he began to beat his wife again. In early January, Mauroy's wife begged Denis to do a third transfusion to try to calm her husband. Denis reluctantly agreed. Mauroy looked much wilder than he had before the first experiment. As the transfusion began, he had a seizure. Within a few hours, he was dead.

Denis was arrested and charged with killing his patient. The transfusions probably did kill Mauroy, but at the time, so little was known about blood that it could not be proved. At Denis's trial, a witness gave evidence suggesting that Mauroy's wife had poisoned her husband. It wasn't strong enough evidence for her to be charged with the crime, but it was enough to get Denis off the hook. He was acquitted.

But the technique of blood transfusion did not recover from this blow. In a way, transfusion itself was found guilty. In 1668 the French court banned transfusions into humans. The Catholic Church and the English Parliament outlawed it soon afterward.

A Few More Tries

Animal-to-animal transfusion was still legal, but few transfusions of any kind were done for 150 years. Then, in 1818, a British physician named James Blundell tried the technique again. His work was different from Lower's and Denis's in two important ways: he transfused only human blood into his patients, and he did the transfusions only to replace blood the patient had lost due to injury or childbirth. He didn't believe transfusion could change someone's character or cure mental illness. The medical community would eventually come to agree with him on this point.

Blundell made huge advances. But germs and blood types were still unknown. Of the ten patients Blundell transfused, half survived and half died. We don't know if the transfusion procedure was responsible for the deaths. It's possible that those patients would have died anyway because of their earlier loss of blood.

During the next few decades, many doctors in Europe and the United States tried transfusion. Their results were similar to Blundell's. Even after the discovery of microbes and the development of sterilization techniques in the 1860s, a large percentage of transfusion recipients died.

James Blundell, a British physician, used transfusion to treat patients with severe bleeding.

MICROBES AND INFECTION

Two of the greatest advances in medicine were the discovery that many diseases are caused by microscopic organisms and the development of techniques to prevent infection during surgery. Both occurred during the mid-1800s.

In the 1840s, Ignaz Semmelweis, a Hungarian doctor, was working in a maternity ward in Vienna. More than 13 percent of the women who gave birth there died of an illness called childbed fever. Semmelweis thought that the doctors were spreading the disease. They were working with cadavers (dead human bodies) and then visiting patients without washing their hands in between. Semmelweis realized the doctors were carrying an infectious agent throughout the ward. He established strict rules for cleanliness and hand washing. The number of patients who died from childbed fever dropped to less than 1 percent.

Ignaz Semmelweis taught medical professionals the importance of scrubbing before visiting patients.

At about the same time in France, chemist Louis Pasteur was studying bacterial contamination of fluids such as broth and milk. Most scientists believed that microbes appeared out of nowhere. But Pasteur proved that a fluid became infested with bacteria only if bacteria had been present in the container or in the air the fluid was exposed to. He showed that contamination could be eliminated by filtering out the microbes, treating them with certain chemicals, or heating the fluid (a process that became known as pasteurization).

In Germany, physician Robert Koch developed the germ theory of disease. This is the idea that specific diseases are caused by specific microbes. He identified the bacteria that cause tuberculosis and anthrax.

In Scotland surgeon Joseph Lister *(below)* put all this evidence together and revolutionized surgical practice. He used carbolic acid (now called phenol) to sterilize instruments before every use. He had his doctors wash their hands in it and wear gloves during surgery. He even sprayed carbolic acid on wounds and bandages, thereby reducing the occurrence of gangrene. He went on to establish antiseptic procedures for operating rooms. These procedures dramatically reduced the number of post-operative infections.

In 1873 Franz Gesellius, a doctor in Poland, reviewed all the transfusions for which he could find records. He found that 56 percent of the patients receiving a transfusion had died soon afterward. The procedure didn't appear to help patients. In many cases, it seemed to do just the opposite. Once again, transfusion fell into disrepute. This time, governments didn't have to ban it. Doctors didn't want to do the procedure anyway. It just didn't seem worth the trouble.

Chapter 4

ANSWERS AT LAST

Lower, Denis, and Blundell firmly believed that blood transfusion could be a powerful healing tool. However, they were unable to overcome two major problems that plagued the technique.

The first problem was that blood clotted in the needles and tubes within five minutes of beginning a transfusion. Then the clots had to be cleared out so the blood could continue flowing into the recipient. That made transfusion awkward and messy. Clotting also meant that blood could not be stored for later use. The donor and the recipient had to be present at the same time.

The other major problem was one they didn't even know they had: that people have different types of blood and the donor and recipient types must match. Mismatched blood was probably the biggest cause of death in transfusions prior to the 1900s. It is almost certainly what killed Antoine Mauroy.

Within the first few years of the twentieth century, doctors would solve both problems. Blood transfusion would finally begin to fulfill its promise as a medical treatment.

Mismatched Blood

Researchers in the 1800s had seen hints that blood from different people might be incompatible. When blood from one person was mixed with blood from another, the fluid often formed gooey gobs. Looking at the gobs through a microscope revealed that the RBCs had clumped together or burst open. The clumping of RBCs is different from clotting. A clot involves platelets and fibrous proteins. A clump is a gob of RBCs stuck together.

Initially, doctors thought clumping was due to illness in one of the people whose blood was being tested. But in 1900 an Austrian doctor named Karl Landsteiner noticed RBC clumps in mixtures of blood from healthy people. That struck him as odd. If clumping was due to illness, then the two samples should have mixed with no problem.

Intrigued, Landsteiner gathered blood samples from twenty-two healthy people who worked in his lab, including himself. He let the samples sit until the RBCs settled to the bottom, drew off the plasma, and mixed each person's RBCs with another person's plasma. Then he watched to see if the RBCs clumped.

Some of the samples clumped, and some didn't. The samples fell into three categories, which Landsteiner labeled A, B, and C. Plasma from group A clumped RBCs from group B, and plasma from group B clumped RBCs from group A. Plasma from group

Karl Landsteiner, an Austrian-born physician, discovered that humans have several different blood types.

C clumped RBCs from both A and B. RBCs from group C didn't clump no matter what plasma they were exposed to.

To Landsteiner, the clumping looked like an immune reaction. He knew that antibodies could bind to antigens, proteins that were foreign to the body. Each kind of antibody recognized and bound to one kind of antigen, and the antibody-antigen combination formed a clump. Landsteiner correctly guessed that antibodies in the plasma were binding to antigens on some of the RBCs. RBCs of other samples were not recognized as foreign, so they didn't clump. Based on the clumping pattern he saw, Landsteiner concluded that humans have three main blood types: A, B, and C. He later changed the name C to O to signify that the third group's RBCs did not clump. Workers in his lab would find a fourth type, dubbed AB, in a larger experiment two years later.

Landsteiner knew that his work explained why so many people died after receiving a transfusion. If donated blood wasn't the right type, the recipient's antibodies would attack the donor's RBCs. If the attack caused the red cells to clump, they could block small blood vessels and cause a heart attack or stroke. If it caused hemolysis, the bursting of RBCs, their contents would be dumped into the bloodstream. RBC contents can be deadly if they are released. Free hemoglobin in the bloodstream damages the kidneys. It also turns urine black, which is often the first visible sign that RBCs have been damaged. Bits of RBCs clog the capillaries. Other substances damage thin vessel walls, leading to nosebleeds and other bleeding elsewhere in the body.

Landsteiner was right. Humans have a few distinct types of blood, and mixing different types often causes problems that resemble an immune reaction. Yet despite his careful work, for a long time, nobody listened.

Finally, in 1912, Dr. Reuben Ottenberg at Mount Sinai Hospital in New York City read Landsteiner's papers and understood their significance. Ottenberg began matching blood donors with recipients. In 125 transfusions with matched blood, he didn't observe a single reaction of the kind that had killed Mauroy.

Ottenberg also realized that type O blood could be given to people with any blood type and that people with AB blood could safely receive a donation of any other type of blood. He called type O people universal donors and type AB people universal recipients.

Despite Ottenberg's support, the medical community was slow to accept blood grouping. Matching donors and recipients didn't become standard practice until the 1920s. By then Landsteiner had come to work at the Rockefeller Institute for Medical Research in New York. In 1929 he became a U.S. citizen. In 1930 he was awarded the Nobel Prize in Medicine for his visionary work.

Dr. Reuben Ottenberg was the first doctor in the United States to introduce blood typing and matching before transfusion.

PERCENT OF PEOPLE IN THE UNITED STATES WITH EACH BLOOD TYPE

Blood type	Percent	Equivalent to
O+	37.4	1 in 3
A+	35.7	1 in 3
B+	8.5	1 in 12
O−	6.6	1 in 15
A−	6.3	1 in 16
AB+	3.4	1 in 29
B−	1.5	1 in 67
AB−	0.6	1 in 167

 Blood Groups

Type A and type B cells have different kinds of sugars attached to the proteins on their surface. These sugars are the antigens that cause incompatibility between different blood types. Type AB cells have both the A and the B antigens. Type O cells have neither. The A and B antigens are found on all of the kinds of cells in the body, not just RBCs. Our blood always carries antibodies against ABO antigens we don't have. With most other antigens, our bodies make antibodies only after we have been exposed to an antigen. ABO blood-type antibodies are different. We are born with antibodies to the antigens of blood types different from our own.

Blood types are inherited. You get one ABO gene from each parent. If you're type A, you have either two A genes or an A and an O. Your cells bear the type A antigen, and your blood carries antibodies against the type B antigen. If you're type B, you have either two B genes or a B and an O. Your cells bear the type B antigen, and your blood carries antibodies against the type A antigen. If you're type AB, you have an A gene and a B gene. Your cells bear both type A and type B antigens, and your blood doesn't carry antibodies to either. If you're type O, you have two O genes. Your cells don't bear either the A or the B antigen, and your blood carries antibodies against both. These antibodies sometimes cause a problem when type O blood is given to someone of a different type. Unless a large amount of blood is transfused, however, the amount of antibody is small enough that the recipient has just a mild reaction.

Another kind of blood antigen that can cause problems for people receiving a transfusion is Rh factor. Landsteiner helped discover it in 1939. More than fifty different variations in the Rh factor exist. Two of them, called Rh-D-positive and Rh-D-negative, are especially important in blood transfusion. (Usually these names are shortened by leaving out the *D*.) Whether you are Rh-positive or Rh-negative depends on whether or not your red blood cells carry the D antigen on their surface. Your Rh type shows up as a "+" or a "−" after your ABO type. Your blood type might be A+ or O−, for example.

Rh-positive people can receive Rh-negative blood with no problem. If you're Rh-negative, you can accept just one transfusion of Rh-positive blood. After that you must receive only Rh-negative blood, because your first exposure to Rh-positive blood will have caused your immune system to make anti-Rh-D antibodies. If you were to receive a second dose of Rh-positive blood, your antibodies would attack the donated red blood cells, making them clump together or burst open.

WHEN MOTHER AND BABY DON'T MATCH

Like ABO blood types, the Rh blood type is inherited. If you receive the Rh+ gene from one or both parents, you will be Rh-positive. If you receive the Rh– gene from both parents, you will be Rh-negative.

The Rh blood type is especially important when an Rh-negative mother gives birth to Rh-positive babies. That can happen if an Rh-positive father passes the Rh+ gene along to his children. The first baby will be fine. A developing fetus has its own blood cells, and its blood stays separate from the mother's blood. But when the mother gives birth, she is exposed to some of the baby's blood. Her immune system recognizes the Rh-positive protein as foreign, and makes antibodies to destroy it.

Since the baby has already been born, it is safely out of reach of the antibodies. But if the woman gets pregnant with another Rh-positive baby, that baby is in trouble. The mother's anti-Rh antibodies can travel across the placenta, the tissue that connects mother and fetus, and enter the baby's body. There, they will destroy most of the baby's red blood cells. The baby will be born with a very severe form of anemia called hemolytic disease of the newborn. It won't have enough RBCs to carry oxygen to its cells. Unless it receives massive transfusions, the baby will die.

Doctors now recognize more than a dozen different blood antigens in addition to A, B, and the Rh antigens. They rarely cause a problem if they mix during transfusion. We don't usually carry antibodies against these antigens unless we have previously received a transfusion of that kind of blood. Therefore, donated blood is usually not tested for these antigens.

Stubborn Clots

Doctors had struggled to solve the clotting problem ever since Lower first transfused dogs. No matter what they did, soon after the blood was exposed to air, it began to clot.

One way around the clotting problem was to sew the donor's blood vessel directly to the recipient's. Since the donor's blood flowed straight into the recipient without touching air, it didn't clot. The technique was very difficult, though. Many doctors weren't good enough surgeons to do it. It also took a lot of time. This was dangerous for the donor. The part of the body that the donating blood vessel normally carried blood to could suffer damage if it was deprived of oxygen for too long. This approach turned out not to be practical for transfusions, but it was later used to connect transplanted organs to their new blood supply. The doctor who perfected the technique, Alexis Carrel, won the Nobel Prize in 1912 for his surgical wizardry.

A more practical approach was to look for a way to prevent clots from forming whether the blood was exposed to air or not. Researchers found a variety of anticoagulants—chemicals that blocked clot formation. They tried mixing anticoagulants with donated blood, but all of them turned out to be toxic to humans. Some patients even died after receiving blood that had been treated with an anticoagulant.

In 1915 Dr. Richard Lewisohn at Mount Sinai Hospital in New York took another look at an anticoagulant called sodium citrate (or simply citrate). Earlier experiments had shown that it was toxic when used in a 1 percent solution. After many trials, Lewisohn discovered that a 0.2 percent citrate solution prevented clots from forming while having no ill effect on the transfusion recipient. Doctors still use sodium citrate to keep donated blood from clotting.

Putting It All Together

Blood typing solved the problem of donor incompatibility, but it created a new one—finding a matching donor in time to help a patient in need. Before blood typing, a doctor simply asked for a volunteer from the hospital staff. Anyone's blood would do. The need to match blood types made it much harder to find a donor in a hurry.

One early solution tried in New York City in the early 1900s was to pay the donors. Unfortunately, it attracted people who wanted quick cash, often to buy alcohol or drugs. The donors weren't screened for health problems. Some carried diseases such as syphilis, malaria, and hepatitis B. Physicians suspected that transfusion could spread disease, but proof of this was slow in coming. For instance, it wasn't known for sure until 1947 that malaria could be transmitted via blood transfusion.

Doctors soon realized they needed a better approach. They enlisted donors who would be "on call" to give blood whenever their blood type was needed. These donors first had to pass a medical exam, prove they didn't have a drug or alcohol problem, and stay in good health. They also had to have a telephone so doctors could reach them in an emergency. Not everyone could afford a phone back then, so this requirement meant that most donors had a good job and a nice home. "Street people" could no longer make a living by selling their own blood. This system worked well for several years, but it still involved waiting for the donor to arrive. For patients who needed an immediate transfusion, even a short delay could be deadly.

The next advance came a few years later. Researchers found that if they added a kind of sugar called dextrose to donated blood, the RBCs stayed healthy and the blood remained usable for several days after donation. For the first time ever, blood could be stored.

The first doctor to pursue blood storage on a big scale was a Russian, Serge Yudin. He lived in an area where transportation and communication problems made it hard to find donors quickly. Yudin knew he could save more lives if his hospital could stockpile blood to use in emergencies. His solution was to use blood from people who had just died. He chose "donors" who had died in accidents or by violence, rather than from disease. He tested the blood for syphilis and determined its type. He mixed in a little citrate and dextrose and stored the blood in glass bottles in a refrigerator. Then he did an autopsy, a dissection and examination of the donor body, to look for signs of disease. If the person appeared to have been healthy, Yudin accepted the blood for use in a transfusion.

Yudin knew that transfusing cadaver blood was a gamble. Nobody knew if blood remained "healthy" after a person died. It might contain harmful substances that were released at the time of death. Transfusing cadaver blood into a living person was so risky that Yudin waited until he had just the right patient—a young man who had tried to kill himself by cutting his wrists. He was the perfect choice, since he would die without a transfusion, and no other blood was available. The transfusion saved the young man's life.

Yudin went on to do 2,500 transfusions of cadaver blood during the 1930s. About 5 percent of the recipients had minor reactions, such as a fever, and only 7 of them—0.3 percent—died. That was an excellent record for a brand-new procedure.

It compared well with the success rate of transfusions using blood from living donors.

Perhaps Yudin's greatest legacy was the idea of storing large amounts of blood in a central location, for future use by anyone who needed it. In the United States, physician Bernard Fantus read about Yudin's "blood centers" and was inspired to start one—stocked by living donors—at Cook County Hospital in Chicago. Established in 1937, it was the first blood-storage center in the United States. At first Fantus gave it a rather pompous name—the Blood Preservation Laboratory. But as he watched donors leave "deposits," and doctors make "withdrawals," he saw a resemblance to another kind of storage place, and he changed its name. The blood bank was born.

Just in Time

The advances in blood storage came along just in time. In the 1930s, civil war broke out in Spain and Nazi Germany began taking over its smaller neighbors. The world was on the verge of all-out war.

The Spanish Civil War (1936–1939) provided a training ground for transfusion doctors who would later help win World War II (1939–1945) for the Allies. An energetic doctor from Canada, Norman Bethune, went to Spain and started the first mobile blood service. He collected blood from donors in Madrid and carried it to frontline hospitals in a van he outfitted with a kerosene-powered refrigerator. Unfortunately, Bethune didn't know much about storing blood. As his van bumped over the back roads, RBCs in the donated blood broke open. Bethune couldn't see the damage, so he went ahead and transfused the blood. Even though Bethune type-matched blood to

As a doctor in Montreal, Canada, Norman Bethune often gave poor people free medical care.

patient, over a seven-week period, more than half of those who received blood from Bethune's van died. Another quarter of them suffered severe reactions.

A Spanish doctor, Federico Duran-Jorda, realized that charging off down the road with fragile blood cells wasn't the best way to help the patients who needed blood. He stayed in Barcelona and built a blood program that stressed safety. He collected only type O blood that could be given to any patient. He screened all donations for syphilis. And he invented a system of bottles, tubes, and valves that kept the blood from being contaminated by microbes in the air.

When the Nationalist army led by Francisco Franco attacked Barcelona in early 1939, a quarter of a million people fled the city. Duran-Jorda evacuated his clinic and found his way to Great Britain. Dr. Janet Vaughan, a blood expert, invited him to live with her family while he helped her set up a blood program in London. Their team recruited eighty thousand type-O donors just in time to save thousands of people during the siege that became known as the London Blitz. For two months in the fall of 1940, German planes dropped bombs on the British capital almost every night. While Vaughan's blood banks were helping Londoners survive the Blitz, new research in the United States was changing blood transfusion yet again.

Chapter 5

TAKING BLOOD APART

Going into World War II, doctors knew how to collect and store blood and how to match donors with recipients. But the field of blood transfusion was changing fast. It had to. The demand for blood skyrocketed during the war years. Scientists responded by inventing new ways of using the precious resource.

Plasma Magic

During the London Blitz (the bombing of London by Nazi warplanes), many people died after suffering injuries that at first didn't seem to be life threatening. They might have had a leg crushed or sustained a severe burn. A few hours after being hurt, these patients became pale. Their pulse speeded up and got weaker. They felt cold, they gasped for breath, and finally they died.

These symptoms weren't new. Doctors had seen them in earlier wars, and in civilian life too, when a person took a bad fall or got hit by a car. Doctors call these symptoms shock. A patient doesn't have to lose a lot of blood to go into shock. Think of it as a shock to the system—the whole body reacting to a terrible injury. Shock occurs when water oozes out of the blood vessels into surrounding tissues. Blood vessel walls are soft and flexible. They collapse when there's not enough fluid inside the vessel. That makes it hard for the blood to circulate. Then the

This double-decker bus fell into a bomb crater in 1940, during the Nazi bombing of London.

(57)

THIS IS SHOCK

This poster was produced by the U.S. War Department during World War II. It depicts an injured soldier suffering from shock.

heart may give out, or other organs may fail because they can't get the oxygen they need.

As World War II began in Europe, doctors looked for ways to boost the volume of blood in patients who were in shock. Whole blood would work, but it was hard to come by. Whole blood could be stored for a week at most. After that, the RBCs died or broke open. A week wasn't long enough to gather donations in the United States, package them, and ship them to Europe.

Doctors tried injecting shock victims with fluids such as salt solutions, with little success. Then they tried plasma. Dr. John Elliott, of Rowan Hospital in Salisbury, North Carolina, found a quick way to separate the plasma from a sample of donated blood. He used a machine called a centrifuge, which could spin a liquid sample very fast—thousands of times per minute—and quickly force heavier substances to the bottom of the tube. When Elliott spun blood, the cells went to the bottom of the tube. Then he collected the layer of plasma from the top of the sample.

Elliott transfused the plasma into volunteers who had donated blood or suffered a bad injury. He found that it restored their blood volume and prevented the problems that usually occurred with shock. Elliott became convinced that plasma would be as useful as blood for treating shock victims. Plasma was also a much better candidate for transport across the Atlantic. It could be stored for weeks, since it didn't contain RBCs that might go bad. It didn't have to be typed and matched to the recipient. Since plasma contained no cells, the recipient's antibodies wouldn't react against it no matter what type of blood it came from. Plasma from any donor could be given to any recipient. (Plasma contains antibodies that might react against the cells of a nonmatching recipient. In most cases, however, the reaction is mild and does not outweigh the value of the transfusion.)

Plasma for Britain

Elliott's results encouraged the U.S. government to start a program called Plasma for Britain. It was the first program ever designed to ship a blood product overseas. A young doctor named Charles Drew was hired to set up and run the program. He was the first African American to receive a medical degree from New York City's prestigious Columbia University. Drew had done research on blood and plasma, and he was great at organizing large groups of people to do complicated work.

Plasma for Britain was an ambitious project. Since only about half of each unit of blood is plasma, making one unit of plasma

THE AMERICAN RED CROSS

The American Red Cross was established in 1881, under the direction of Clara Barton, who was a nurse during the Civil War (1861–1865). It provides medical supplies and treatment to soldiers and civilians during wartime and to anyone affected by natural disasters such as hurricanes or human-caused tragedies such as terrorist attacks. The Red Cross also offers training in first aid and water safety. It is one of the largest collectors and distributors of blood in the world.

required two units of blood, and Drew needed to produce thousands of units of plasma every week. The American Red Cross ran donation drives to bring in the massive amounts of blood his program needed. Donations poured in, and Drew's "assembly line" pumped out the finished product.

As plasma was used in the field more often, a problem came up. It often got contaminated. Any microbes that happened to get into a bottle or tube of plasma multiplied quickly. A batch of plasma could test "clean" one week and show up as contaminated two weeks later. Patients who received contaminated plasma usually died.

Since bacteria could sneak in through any tiny hole, Drew developed a system of tubes and valves that completely isolated the blood from air. Duran-Jorda had pioneered this approach during the Spanish Civil War. Drew showed that it worked just as well on a much larger scale. Drew also tested every batch of

Charles Drew's methods for preserving and transporting huge amounts of human blood helped save thousands of British citizens during World War II.

plasma several times before shipping it and discarded any plasma that had been contaminated.

During the first two years of World War II, Drew's program sent thousands of units of plasma to Britain. Drew changed the field of blood transfusion forever by introducing assembly-line methods to process huge amounts of blood.

Breaking Blood Apart

While Plasma for Britain sent shiploads of plasma across the Atlantic, scientists kept looking for better ways to treat shock victims. One advance was to turn liquid plasma into a powder by freeze-drying it. The powder didn't get contaminated as easily as liquid plasma did, and it was much easier to handle. An army medic could carry a bottle of powdered plasma and a bottle of sterile water. When a patient needed plasma, the medic simply mixed the two and got perfectly good liquid plasma that was ready to be transfused.

An even bigger advance came from Dr. Edwin Cohn. He was a chemist who specialized in proteins. Cohn thought that if he could separate all the proteins in plasma and test each one alone, he could figure out what each one did. He especially wanted to know whether one of the proteins could be used by itself to treat shock victims.

Cohn found that the proteins dissolved in plasma would precipitate, or "un-dissolve," if he added alcohol to the plasma. Some of the proteins looked grainy, like the "snowflakes" in a snow globe, and others looked wispy. Spinning the sample in a centrifuge sent them to the bottom quickly. Then they could be collected and studied. The problem was that figuring out

In this photo, Edwin Cohn holds a device that could be used to separate whole blood into cells and plasma.

what the proteins were and what they did was nearly impossible with all of them jumbled together.

Cohn's big breakthrough was to figure out how to make the proteins precipitate one or a few at a time, rather than all at once. He knew from his earlier work that different proteins react differently to different conditions. If he could find a way to make some proteins in the plasma remain dissolved while others precipitated out, he could separate them. He used a stepwise process. First, he adjusted the salinity, acidity, and temperature of the plasma. Then he added alcohol. Some of the proteins precipitated. Cohn centrifuged the sample and collected the dense powder at the bottom of the tube. He called it Fraction I. Then he turned his attention to the remaining liquid, which was plasma minus Fraction I. He changed the conditions slightly and added more alcohol. More proteins precipitated. They made up Fraction II. Cohn continued this fractionation process until no more protein appeared when he added alcohol. Then he tested all of the fractions.

Cohn found that Fraction V contained an antishock agent— just what he had been hoping for. When he analyzed it, the white powder turned out to be almost pure albumin. It could be stored indefinitely without breaking down. When it was transfused into a shock patient, each grain of albumin acted like a miniature sponge, drawing water from the surrounding tissues back into the blood vessels.

By December 1941, Cohn's lab had made a small amount of albumin—not quite enough to treat one hundred patients. Cohn planned to do more tests to make sure it was safe for human patients. The Japanese attack on Pearl Harbor, Hawaii, on December 7 changed his plans. He sent all of his albumin to Pearl Harbor with a doctor from his staff, Isadore Ravdin.

When Ravdin arrived on December 11, the hospital itself was in shock. More than two thousand people had already died. Thousands more lay wounded by shrapnel, bullets, and burns. Many patients had received only basic treatment, such as morphine to kill the pain. The doctors and nurses had been working nonstop since the attack. Overwhelmed by the number of casualties, they were reaching their limit.

Ravdin went to work. He transfused albumin into eighty-seven patients—burn victims and others who were so deeply in shock that the other doctors had almost given up on them. The albumin worked. It restored the patients' blood volume and pulled them out of shock. To the overworked doctors and their desperate patients, albumin was a miracle cure.

The U.S. government was so impressed by these results that it commissioned seven drug companies to make more albumin. Cohn supervised the effort. He also continued to study his remaining plasma fractions. Who knew what other wonders he might find there?

Beyond Albumin

When Cohn and his team took a closer look at other plasma fractions, they found a treasure chest of medical marvels. Fraction I contained fibrinogen, which helped patients whose blood didn't clot well or who had been badly injured and were bleeding profusely. Fractions II and III contained many kinds of antibodies. Each kind attacked the microbe that caused a specific disease. Cohn's team found antibodies that fought measles, mumps, and polio. They could be injected to help a person resist a disease for a few weeks or a few months. Fraction IV contained other antibodies and cholesterol, a fatty substance.

The researchers saved the RBCs that they separated from plasma. The RBCs could be transfused into patients to boost their ability to get oxygen to their tissues. People who received plasma or albumin to save them from shock often needed RBCs later, to restore their body's ability to move oxygen.

Cohn was delighted. Transfusing whole blood seemed wasteful to him. If a patient needed only albumin or a clotting factor, why give him whole blood? With fractionation, the patient could receive exactly what he needed and nothing more.

Cohn called the targeted use of blood fractions component therapy because different components of blood were used in very specific ways. Component therapy made efficient use of donated blood, because it allowed each pint to help several different patients. If they weren't fractionated, four units of whole blood could be transfused into just four people. With plasma separation, four units of blood provided four units of RBCs and two units of plasma, which could help six patients. With full fractionation, four units of blood provided a variety of components that could help twenty-three patients.

The Blood Factory

During its peak years, Cohn's lab looked like a superclean factory. Pipes and tubes connected dozens of big vats. Gauges kept track of temperature and pressure. Refrigerators hummed and centrifuges whirred. The lab ran twenty-four hours a day, turning whole blood into six blood products ready for transfusion into patients.

The only time the lab slowed down was when it ran out of blood. Cohn urged the American Red Cross to send more. The Red Cross started blood drives all over the country to encourage

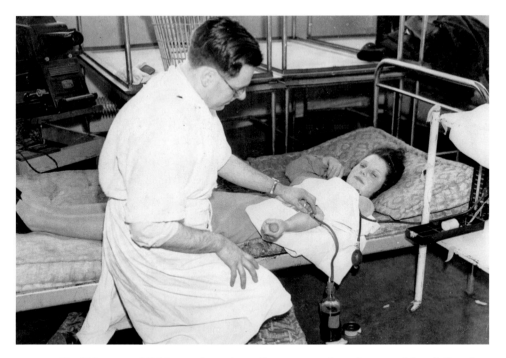

In February 1944, an American factory worker donates blood for the war effort.

people to donate. Businesses and clubs competed to see which could provide the most blood. Posters and newsreels showed celebrities donating. Soldiers who had been saved by transfusions wrote testimonials about their experience. Soon giving blood was seen as a patriotic duty, something the people at home could do to support their sons and husbands who were fighting overseas.

The demand for blood shot up from 250,000 pints in 1942 to more than 1,000,000 pints in 1943—and the blood drives were able to meet the demand. Cohn's lab kept churning out blood products for the patients who needed them.

U.S. Army medics transfuse plasma into a soldier wounded off the coast of Normandy, France, in June 1944.

After the War

When World War II ended, the U.S. government and drug companies shut down many blood labs. But the drop in demand didn't last long. The ability to collect large amounts of blood and to fractionate it into useful products led to many new treatments and procedures.

Open-heart surgery and organ transplantation became possible because doctors now had a way to deal with the massive loss of blood caused by the operations. Another advance was chemotherapy—the use of powerful chemicals to fight cancer. Patients going through chemotherapy often suffered internal bleeding, as the drugs impaired their blood's ability to clot.

Transfusing them with platelets and clotting factors helped them survive their cancer treatments.

Another important invention came along in 1950—the plastic storage bag. Storing and shipping blood became much easier and safer. RBCs didn't break open in plastic bags, as they often did in glass bottles, because they didn't stick to plastic. RBCs tended to stick so tightly to glass that the cells broke open. Plastic bags also took up less space than glass bottles, and they weren't breakable. In fact, they passed the government's ultimate toughness test—being dropped out of an airplane 2,000 feet (600 meters) above the ground!

Component Therapy

In the years since Cohn invented plasma fractionation, blood researchers have continued to further fractionate blood to find new and useful blood components. At least twenty different fractions of blood are used to treat patients. Patients almost never receive whole blood anymore. Getting too much fluid can cause a condition called circulatory overload, which makes the heart work too hard and can kill the recipient. The first transfusionists had been right to drain a little blood out of a patient before performing a transfusion!

A patient who has lost a lot of blood is given RBCs so her tissues can keep getting the oxygen they need. Fresh frozen plasma contains all of the clotting factors. It is a lifesaver for people whose blood won't clot right for any reason. Factor VIII, or antihemophilic factor (AHF), gives people with hemophilia A the specific clotting substance their bodies cannot make. Factor IX helps people with hemophilia B, and factor XI helps those with hemophilia C. Other components are used to treat patients with other hereditary blood diseases, severe burns, or liver disease.

Blood as a Business

Researchers continued to explore how to use blood components. They began to think of blood the way oil companies view crude oil, which can be made into gasoline, diesel fuel, or plastic. Blood became a raw material for a brand-new industry.

Treating blood and blood components as products was good in some ways. The companies became very efficient at collecting and distributing blood to more and more people all over the globe. It was not so good in other ways. Sometimes blood suppliers focused on quantity more than on quality. Then medical aspects of blood, such as safety, took second place to the business aspects, such as boosting production.

From the 1940s to the 1980s, people looked at blood in three ways. Scientists viewed blood as a complex substance that performed certain jobs in the body. Businesses viewed blood as a resource they could sell. Most ordinary people were a bit confused about blood and transfusion. They knew transfusion could save lives. But their minds harbored old superstitions and fears about blood. While all of these ideas swirled through the culture, within the blood itself lurked new and deadly dangers.

Chapter 6

OLD FEARS, NEW DANGERS

On a cold Monday afternoon in 1942, a young African American woman walked into the local Red Cross blood center. She felt numb, but not from the cold. That morning she had received a telegram from the U.S. Army. Her husband, an army private, had been badly wounded in battle in Germany. Unable to help him directly, she decided there was one thing she could do to help some other soldier instead. She would give blood.

But when she got to the blood center, she was turned away. The blood center accepted blood from African Americans only on Fridays, she was told. That way they could keep it separate from white people's blood.

Race and Blood

The United States' first big plasma program had been launched by an African American doctor, Charles Drew. Edwin Cohn's fractionation work was showing that every unit of blood had the same basic ingredients, no matter who it came from. Some blood types were more common in some races than in others, but a person from any race or ethnic group might have any blood type. Yet in the 1940s and 1950s, many people clung to the notion that "white blood" was better than "black blood."

In 1959 a blood bank official in Little Rock, Arkansas, holds bottles of blood labeled with the donors' race.

This wasn't the view of some fringe group. It was the official policy of the U.S. government and the American Red Cross.

All donations from nonwhites were labeled so they could be kept separate from blood that came from white donors. African Americans could be given blood from anyone, but white people were supposed to be transfused only with "white blood." Even Dr. Drew's blood would have been labeled and set apart for use only in an African American recipient.

Fortunately for wounded U.S. soldiers during World War II, the policy didn't create a shortage of blood. There were usually enough white donors to provide all the blood they needed, and in the chaos of military hospitals near the front lines, doctors sometimes ignored the rules. They knew that a soldier who was bleeding to death could be saved by blood from anybody.

German soldiers weren't so lucky. The Nazis who controlled Germany believed that their ethnic group was superior to all others, including Jews, Poles, Russians, and the Dutch. Members of these "inferior" groups were not allowed to donate blood for transfusion into German patients. By refusing to accept blood from them, German blood banks ran short. Over the course of the war, thousands of German soldiers died for lack of a simple blood transfusion.

Some U.S. blood centers continued to segregate the blood of black and white donors until the 1960s, but superstitious fears about the donor's race gradually faded. In their place came fear of something much more real.

A New Threat

In 1980 a young married couple in California found out they were going to have a second baby. Tests showed the fetus was

Rh-positive. That was a problem, because the mother was Rh-negative and had already had an Rh-positive child. Her anti-Rh antibodies destroyed the fetus's RBCs. When he was born, the baby was severely anemic. Doctors gave him transfusions to keep him alive until his system could make enough of its own RBCs. They replaced his entire volume of blood six times in four days. During the baby's first month of life, he received whole blood, RBCs, and platelets from nineteen different donors.

Finally, the baby was able to go home with his parents, but he soon began having problems. At seven months of age, he got some unusual infections. Later, he suffered from anemia and his immune system failed. He appeared to have the frightening new disease called AIDS.

In the early 1980s, Patrick Burk, a hemophiliac, contracted the HIV virus through clotting factor transfusions. He unknowingly transmitted the virus to his wife, Lauren. Their son, Dwight, was born with AIDS.

This baby's case of AIDS was the first one that doctors were sure was caused by infected blood. They'd had hints before that AIDS could be transmitted through blood transfusion, but they hadn't been able to pin it down. At the time, doctors didn't know that AIDS was caused by a virus. HIV wouldn't be discovered until 1984. Doctors knew that AIDS was usually spread by having sex without a condom (especially among homosexual men) or by sharing injection needles. Those routes hinted that AIDS might also be carried in blood. Looking back through the baby's medical records, doctors found that no one in his family had AIDS or had ever been exposed to AIDS. But one of the donors who provided platelets for the newborn developed AIDS himself several months after donating. The baby could only have gotten the disease from this donor's platelets. Both the donor and the baby eventually died of AIDS.

Bad Blood

Doctors had known for years that some diseases could be transmitted in blood. Some disease organisms—bacteria, parasites, and viruses—live inside blood cells. Others float free in the bloodstream. When blood from an infected person is transfused, the organisms go with it. Then they infect the recipient.

Since large-scale transfusion began in the 1920s, blood banks have tested their donated blood for syphilis. The bacterium that causes syphilis normally passes from person to person through sexual contact, but it also spreads through transfusion of blood from an infected person.

Another bloodborne disease challenged doctors during World War II. Thousands of U.S. soldiers stationed in tropical areas suffered from malaria, which is caused by a tiny parasite

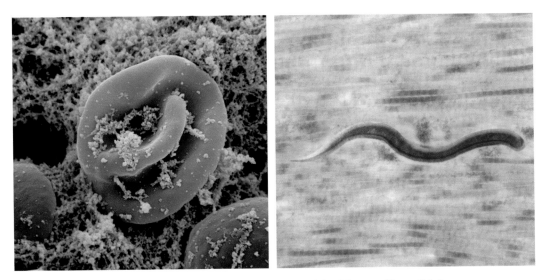

Left: *This red blood cell has been infected by* Plasmodium falciparum *parasites, which cause malaria.* Right: *Spiral-shaped* Treponema pallidum *bacteria cause syphilis.*

that is injected into the bloodstream by a mosquito's bite. Doctors didn't test blood for malaria, but they made an effort to protect transfusion recipients by screening the donors. Doctors didn't accept blood donations from anyone who had had malaria or had been in areas where malaria was common. This screening process wasn't completely effective, however. Malaria has a lag time, which means symptoms don't show up right after infection. Eight days to six months may pass before an infected person becomes sick.

AIDS and other viral diseases, such as hepatitis B and hepatitis C, were even tougher to deal with. A person can be infected with one of these viruses for years before showing any signs of being sick. All during that time, the person's blood carries the virus. If the person donates blood, the virus is "donated" too. That's what happened to the baby in California. Many doctors sounded an alarm when they saw the link between transfusion and AIDS. Blood had become a big business. Transfusion had the potential to infect millions of people.

Fractionation factories pooled plasma from 100,000 different donors for a single production run. If just one donor was infected, the entire pool, and all the components made from it, would be tainted. If that weren't bad enough, the way blood companies collected their raw material practically guaranteed their products would be tainted. Volunteer donors didn't provide enough plasma to keep the factories running, so blood companies opened collection centers in run-down areas of big cities and paid people for their blood. This practice attracted donors who were much more likely to carry HIV than volunteer donors were. Most paid donors were in poor health. Few practiced safe sex by using condoms. Many were drug addicts.

In France, government-run blood banks collected blood from prison convicts. The blood-donation program was seen as a way to let prisoners contribute to society. The prison donors weren't screened at all. Even though one doctor found that almost one-third of the prisoners carried hepatitis B and were at risk of carrying AIDS, they were all allowed to give blood—which was then given to patients throughout France.

The System Fails

Between 1978 and 1986, about twenty thousand Americans contracted AIDS after receiving a transfusion of tainted blood or blood components. Some of the infections happened before doctors knew the disease could be transmitted in blood. But almost all of the infections after 1981 could have been prevented.

Donor questionnaires would have screened out about 85 percent of high-risk donors, but blood centers refused to use them. They felt that asking detailed questions about their donors' sex lives and drug use discriminated against some donors and violated their privacy.

In March 1985, a U.S. company developed a way to test blood for HIV. The test was adopted within a few weeks by blood centers in the United States. The governments of France and Great Britain, however, didn't allow it to be used right away. They delayed for months, until French and British companies could develop their own tests. In the meantime, their citizens continued to receive untested blood products.

While U.S. blood banks adopted the HIV test right away, they only used it on newly donated blood. Blood products already on the shelf were not tested. They were transfused into patients—and the patients were never told they were getting a risky product. Some patients were infected with HIV after receiving tainted products the test would have caught.

People with hemophilia were hit especially hard by the use of untested products. Ryan White, a boy from Indiana, was one victim. Like all hemophiliacs, Ryan's blood lacked a key clotting factor, so it wouldn't clot normally. Even bumping a table or stubbing his toe caused painful bleeding into his joints or around his organs. Ryan relieved his symptoms by injecting factor VIII, a clotting factor that had been made from pooled plasma. Factor VIII helped Ryan live a fairly normal life—until HIV found its way into the nation's blood supply.

The companies and government agencies that handled clotting factors had millions of dollars invested in the products. They didn't want to throw away their entire inventory simply because some of it might be tainted. Even after the HIV test

Ryan White, a hemophiliac who contracted AIDS through clotting factor transfusions

became available, they continued to sell untested clotting factors to Ryan White and others who needed them. They didn't tell the patients that there might be something wrong with the clotting factors. Instead, they reassured hemophiliacs that their clotting factors were safe to use.

By late 1985, donor screening and blood tests for HIV were in place in the United States, Europe, and Japan. But it was too late for Ryan White and for thousands of other people who had received blood products in the previous few years. Ryan was diagnosed with AIDS in 1984. Until his death in 1990, at the age of eighteen, he worked to educate people about HIV and AIDS.

Worldwide, more than forty thousand hemophiliacs—about

half of all the hemophiliacs on Earth—had been infected with HIV. Since they had not been told they were at risk, they hadn't taken precautions to keep from spreading the disease to others. Many of their spouses and loved ones also fell prey to AIDS.

Getting It Right

After the AIDS disaster, government agencies, companies, and blood banks set up new procedures to keep the blood supply safe. In the United States, the Department of Health and Human Services requires blood banks to screen all donors and test all donated blood for the diseases for which tests are available. Blood centers must notify donors whose blood tests positive for any disease, and all donors are asked to notify the blood center if they get sick after donating. Because some diseases have a long lag time, some donors later develop diseases even though their blood tested negative. People who received blood from such donors are informed so they can seek medical help.

The Centers for Disease Control and Prevention (CDC), a federal health agency in Atlanta, Georgia, gathers reports from doctors all over the country about symptoms that might be related to transfusion. They hope to catch any new problems early, before many people are affected. They also keep a close watch on hemophiliacs and others who use blood products often. If there is a new problem in the blood supply, it shows up in them first.

Scientists have added new tests to the safety guidelines periodically, such as when a new disease has been linked to blood products. When a good test for hepatitis C became available in 1990, blood banks applied it to the blood already in their inventory as well as to all new donations.

A scary new disease we don't yet have a test for is variant Creutzfeldt-Jakob disease, or vCJD. It is similar to bovine spongiform encephalopathy (BSE), a disease of cattle commonly known as mad cow disease. Prions, proteins that destroy brain cells, probably cause vCJD. We know that a person can catch vCJD by eating meat from a cow infected with BSE. Doctors think a person probably can become infected by receiving blood products from an infected donor, but they aren't completely sure yet. This disease is very difficult to trace. Its lag time can be longer than thirty years! When vCJD showed up in Great Britain in the mid-1990s, U.S. blood centers began to screen out donors who had lived in Great Britain or eaten British beef during the years 1980 to 1996, when British cows had a high rate of BSE infection.

Trusting Transfusion

In countries that use the new safeguards, the risk of catching AIDS from a blood product is about one in two million. That's much lower than the risk of dying in an auto accident. It's also lower than the risk of catching AIDS by having sex without a condom with someone who has not tested negative for the disease. If blood banks follow the guidelines for screening and testing, receiving a transfusion today is safer than it has ever been before.

Donating blood continues to be safe, as it has been ever since doctors started using sterilized needles. Nobody ever caught AIDS—or any other bloodborne disease—by giving blood at a well-run, modern collection center. Giving blood is one of the safest medical procedures around—and one of the best things a healthy person can do for his or her community.

RECIPE FOR DISASTER

People in many poor African, South American, and Asian countries still can't count on the safety of their blood supply. Their blood collection centers are so poorly equipped that many can't sterilize equipment such as needles. Some don't even have a refrigerator in which to store donated blood—or a reliable source of electricity to power a fridge.

Few of the blood banks in these countries screen all the blood they bring in. Disease tests require expensive supplies and highly trained technicians, which are rare in countries where the average adult earns just a few dollars a day. In such places, blood collection centers might test donations on only one day each week. It may seem that testing some blood is better than testing none at all. But since much donated blood is pooled in big batches to make components, testing just a few of the donations doesn't make sense. "Safe" blood becomes unsafe as soon as it is mixed with disease-carrying blood.

As a result, transfusion in these countries often turns the "gift of life" into a death sentence. In India less than 10 percent of the blood supply is safe. In neighboring Pakistan, nearly half of all current cases of AIDS can be traced to a transfusion of tainted blood. Many more people will be infected and will die unless the blood collection systems in developing countries can be made as safe as those in the United States and other developed countries.

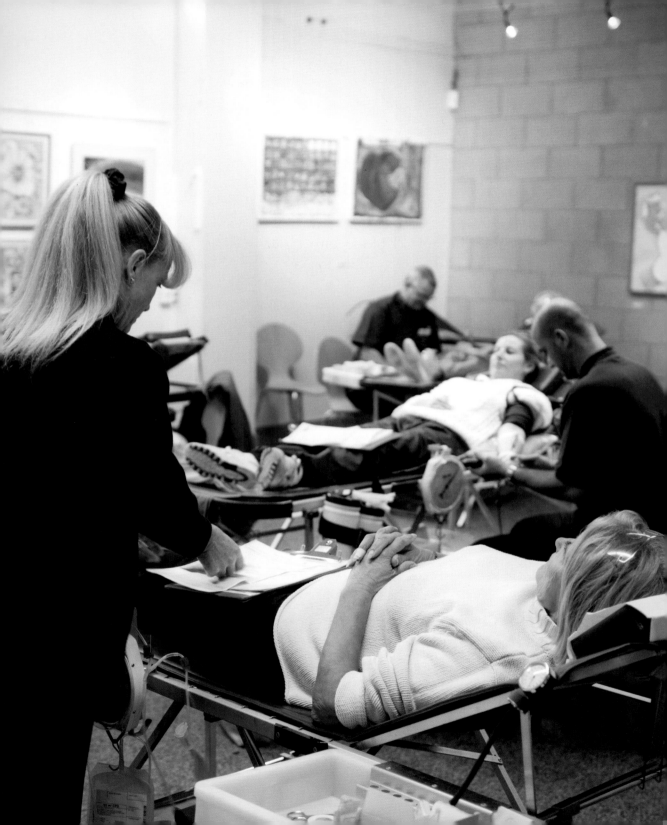

Chapter 7

TWENTY-FIRST CENTURY BLOOD TRANSFUSION

Blood transfusion has changed tremendously since Lower and Denis first put animal blood into human veins. If you give blood, you will do it in a collection center or a bloodmobile, a van that travels around the community to gather donations. Wherever you donate, the floors and countertops will be clean, all the blood-collection instruments will have been sterilized, and there won't be a lamb or cow in sight.

When You Give Blood

Before you give blood, you'll get a quick health check and interview from a phlebotomist, a person who is specially trained in the collection of blood. These steps guarantee your safety by making sure you are healthy enough to lose a unit of blood. They also guarantee the safety of whoever might get your blood, by making sure you haven't been exposed to blood-borne diseases.

In most cases, for your own safety, you must be at least seventeen years old and weigh at least 110 pounds (50 kg) to donate blood. The usual amount collected is one unit, which is equal to 1 pint (0.5 l).

The phlebotomist will check your pulse, temperature, and

Phlebotomists (in blue shirts) collect blood from donors (lying down).

blood pressure. She'll prick your finger to get a drop of blood to test whether you have enough iron-containing hemoglobin. If you don't, you're anemic and you won't be allowed to donate. The phlebotomist will refer you to a doctor who can treat your anemia.

Next comes an interview. If you're obviously sick, the blood center won't accept you as a donor. What's tricky is that you could be infected even if you appear perfectly healthy. Many bloodborne diseases can lurk within the body for months or years before making the person visibly sick.

The phlebotomist will ask you a series of yes/no questions to find out if you might be carrying such a disease. Have you recently gotten a tattoo or a skin piercing? Have you traveled to Africa or lived in Great Britain for more than a few months? Have you injected drugs, including steroids, even once? Have you had sex, even once, with someone who might have injected drugs or with a man who might have had sex with another man?

A yes answer to any of these questions means that you might have been exposed to AIDS, hepatitis C, or other diseases. If you answer yes, you may be declined or deferred as a donor.

Declined means "No, thank you." Some conditions, such as having AIDS, will keep you from ever donating blood. If you are deferred, the center won't accept your blood now, but it will in the future if your health continues to be good. The length of the deferment depends on what you said yes to. People who have had a tattoo or skin piercing must wait one year after that procedure before they can donate. People who have lived in an area where malaria occurs must wait for three years.

Both tattooing and body piercing involve breaking the skin. If the instruments used for these procedures aren't properly sterilized, they can transmit bloodborne diseases.

You'll also be asked about medications you have taken recently. Some would not be good for the recipient of your blood. Donated blood containing Accutane, a drug used to fight acne, could harm a developing baby if it was transfused into a pregnant woman. You'll have to wait until four weeks after you stop taking Accutane before you will be accepted as a blood donor.

Needles and Tubes

Your interview will take just a few minutes. Then it's off to the phlebotomy room. You'll recline in a big padded chair. The phlebotomist will tie a tourniquet around your upper arm and ask you to squeeze a ball or dowel to make your vein pop up. She'll sterilize the skin over your vein before inserting the needle. It might be a little uncomfortable, but it shouldn't hurt, squirt, or ooze blood. Then the phlebotomist will tape the needle to your arm so it doesn't wiggle around or fall out.

The needle comes already connected to the plastic tubing that carries your blood into a sturdy plastic bag. The whole system is closed—air never enters any part of it. The inner surface of the bag is coated with citrate to keep the blood from clotting. The tubing and bag are labeled with your name and an identity code. You'll be given a card with the code on it, so you can call the blood center if you become sick in the days after you donate. The same code will be put on every product that comes from your blood. If a problem shows up with any of them, doctors can trace the blood back to you. They will let

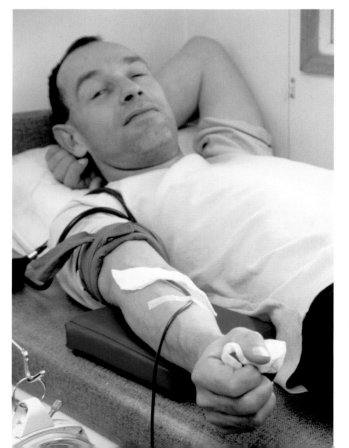

This blood donor is squeezing a rubber ball to encourage good blood circulation in his arm.

you know what they found, so that you can get treatment. They will also track down all the other components made from your blood, so other people don't get infected.

The donation procedure takes thirty minutes at most. Some people's blood flows so quickly that they're done in less than ten minutes. Then the phlebotomist will clamp off the tube that carries your blood to the bag. She'll fill several small, labeled test tubes with your blood. Then she'll remove the needle from your arm, press a cotton ball over the hole, and wrap it with elastic gauze.

Sometimes donors feel lightheaded right after they give blood. Loss of that amount of blood results in less oxygen going to the brain. You should stay in the blood center for at least another ten minutes to let your system adjust to having less blood. The phlebotomist will give you juice and cookies to boost the nutrients in your bloodstream. Over the next few hours, you shouldn't do anything strenuous, such as sports practice or heavy lifting. You should drink plenty of water or juice to replace the fluid you lost.

Your system will replace the plasma you lost within a day. It will take several weeks to replace the RBCs and white cells. You will be able to donate again in eight weeks.

That's all there is to it. You've become a blood donor!

What Happens to the Blood You Donate

After you make your donation, the phlebotomist starts processing your blood. Some samples are tested for blood type. Others are tested for specific diseases.

Your blood will be typed every time you donate. Typing is done in two ways. Forward typing mixes a small sample of your blood with serum from type A and another small sample with

A bag of donated type O-positive blood

serum from type B blood. (Some blood centers also mix a third sample with type AB serum.) Incompatible serum will make your RBCs clump or break open. Just to be sure, the opposite test will also be done. Reverse typing mixes your serum with RBCs from type A and type B blood. Again, compatible serum and RBCs mix with no problem. If the serum and RBCs are not compatible, the RBCs will clump or burst. The results from the two tests should give the same answer. If they don't, your blood will be set aside until the lab investigates further.

Next come the disease tests. In the United States, all donated blood is tested for syphilis, hepatitis B, hepatitis C, HIV, and HTLV I and II (two forms of human T-cell lymphotropic virus, which can cause a form of leukemia). Some centers also test for West Nile virus and cytomegalovirus (CMV). CMV infects monocytes and neutrophils. Most healthy people will not catch CMV from a transfusion, but newborns or people with weak

This bag of blood has been spun in a centrifuge to separate the blood cells from the plasma.

immune systems may get infected. A negative result on a test means the blood does not carry that disease. If all the tests come back negative, your blood can safely be given to patients who need it. If a test comes back positive, your blood is tested again for that disease. If the follow-up test is also positive, your blood will be discarded and you will be told so that you can seek treatment.

Almost all blood that is accepted for transfusion is separated into RBCs and plasma. Sometimes the platelets are separated out too. The blood center uses a centrifuge to separate the components in each unit of blood while it is still in the collection bag. A special instrument pinches the bag to separate it into three small chambers, one for each of the main components. Then the components are stored until they are needed by a patient. Platelets are kept at room temperature because they don't survive long after transfusion if they have been refrigerated. They last only five days. RBCs are refrigerated and will last for forty-two days. Plasma is frozen and will stay effective for one year.

KEEPING THE BLOOD BANKS FULL

Keeping blood banks fully stocked with blood is difficult. Of all Americans who could donate blood, only 5 percent do so. Banks often run short of types O and B blood—O because it is used for transfusion into people of all blood types and B because few donors have type B blood. (Few donors have type AB, either, but since people with type AB blood can receive a transfusion of any other type of blood, maintaining a supply of AB blood is not as crucial.) Supplies of all types of blood drop during the summer and midwinter holidays, when many potential donors are on vacation and don't donate as often.

One thing that always brings in new donors is a disaster. After the terrorist attacks of September 11, 2001, for example, people all over the United States donated their blood. Most had never donated before. There weren't enough patients to use all the blood, though. It sat in storage until it expired forty-two days after donation. Then it was destroyed. U.S. blood banks discarded more than 40,000 units of blood in the winter of 2001. A few months later, they had shortages again. Many of the people who donated right after the attacks never went back to donate again.

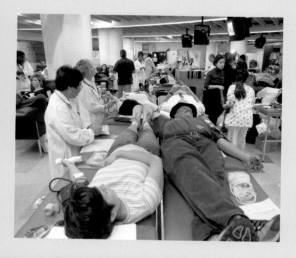

Thousands of people donated blood after the terrorist attacks of September 11, 2001.

When You Receive a Blood Transfusion

If you are one of the 12 million Americans who will need a transfusion at some point in their life, here's how it will work. Just as with donation, the room will be clean and the instruments used will be sterile. The skin on your arm will be carefully cleaned before the needle is inserted into your vein. The bag of plasma, RBCs, or platelets will hang from a hook above your bed, so gravity can help move the product into your vein.

Before hooking up the bag, your doctor or nurse will check your blood type. In addition to matching the types on the bag's labels, your blood will be cross-matched with the donor blood by mixing a few drops of your plasma or serum with donor RBCs. If they're compatible, nothing will happen. If they are not compatible, the RBCs will clump or burst. A quick look through a microscope will reveal what happened.

Donated blood (in the bags) is cross-matched with the intended recipient to make sure it is compatible.

If you're having an operation that was planned in advance, the surgeon will have ordered and cross-matched the blood ahead of time. Some patients who are planning to have surgery donate blood for themselves ahead of time, in a process called autologous donation. That's the surest way to get blood that is compatible and safe. It came from you, after all!

Even if you receive only plasma, it will be cross-matched with your blood type. Unmatched plasma might or might not cause a problem. It wouldn't contain cells that your antibodies could destroy, but it would contain antibodies that might attack your cells. Using matched plasma is safer.

The transfusion will start slowly. If you show any sign of a reaction against the blood, such as a rise in temperature or pain in your arm, your nurse will stop the transfusion. He'll recheck your blood type. He may try again with a different bag of matching blood. If all goes well during the first few minutes of the transfusion, he'll turn a valve to make the blood flow faster. It will take two or three hours for the entire unit of blood to enter your system.

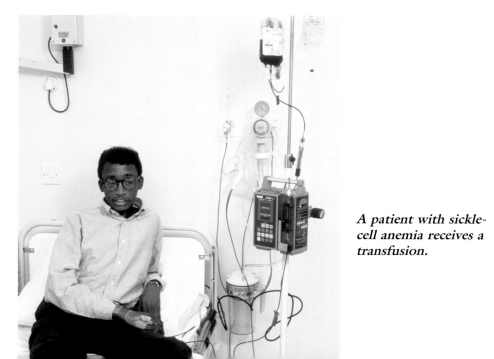

A patient with sickle-cell anemia receives a transfusion.

How much blood you'll need depends on what injury or operation you have. Heart surgery usually requires two units of RBCs, but if you've been taking anticlotting medications, you might need several units of platelets as well. Severe injuries, such as those you might sustain in a car crash, can require up to fifty units of RBCs.

Once it is in your vessels, the donated blood will behave as if it is your own blood. Like your own blood, it will eventually be replaced as your system makes new cells and new plasma proteins.

Bleeding as a Treatment

As doctors have learned more about blood and health, they have found that ancient physicians weren't always wrong. In some cases, bleeding the patient is the best treatment available.

Leeches are used to draw excess blood out of body parts whose veins are so damaged that blood can't flow out. If blood can't drain out of the tissues, they will be damaged and could die. A doctor will place one or a few leeches on the swollen part, and the leeches will bite through the skin and begin feeding. It doesn't hurt, because the leeches inject a mild anesthetic when they bite. They also inject an anticoagulant. After drinking a few milliliters of blood, the leeches fall off. But the tiny wounds continue to bleed for up to ten hours, releasing up to 5 ounces (150 ml) of blood. Usually leeches are used for just a few days. By then the damaged veins have healed.

In a technique called therapeutic apheresis, blood is drawn out of the body and run through a machine that removes harmful substances. Then the "cleaned-up" blood is returned to the patient. This method is used to lower the number of leukocytes in leukemia patients, the number of platelets in

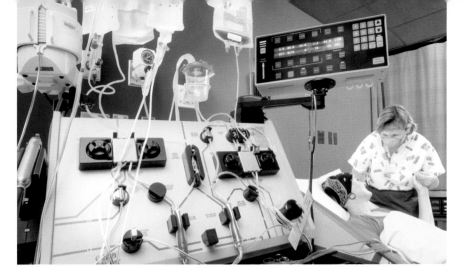

An apheresis machine filters stem cells out of the blood of a cancer patient. Stem cells are special cells that can divide to produce other kinds of cells, such as RBCs, white blood cells, and platelets. The patient's stem cells will be stored and then returned to her blood after she receives chemotherapy, a treatment that will destroy many of her own blood-forming cells along with the cancer cells.

people whose blood clots too easily, and harmful foreign proteins that cause allergic reactions.

Bleeding is the main treatment for hemochromatosis, a condition in which the body stores too much iron. We need a small amount of iron in our systems, but if we have too much, we can suffer arthritis (pain and swelling in the joints), fatigue, and liver damage. People diagnosed with hemochromatosis will have a unit or two of blood removed every week until their iron levels drop. Some people reach normal iron levels after just a few donations. Others may need to lose one hundred units. After that, they need to give blood just a few times a year to keep their iron levels in the safe range.

By the time you read this book, blood banks might be using new procedures. The overall goal will remain the same, however—to allow people to give blood without pain and receive it without fear.

Chapter 8

THE FUTURE OF TRANSFUSION

As our understanding of blood grows, the field of transfusion medicine continues to change. Here are some current areas of transfusion research.

Making the Match

When a patient needs a transfusion immediately and there's not enough time to type his blood or when a blood bank runs out of a particular type of blood, the need to match donor and recipient can be a big problem. Blood banks deal with these situations by stocking up on O-negative blood. That's the universal donor type that can safely be given to anyone in an emergency. But only about 7 percent of all Americans have O-negative blood—not enough to meet the entire demand for blood.

O-positive blood can safely be transfused into anyone with an Rh-positive blood type, but not into someone who is Rh-negative. The ultimate goal is to have blood that can safely be transfused into anyone, without having to verify the blood type of the recipient first. This is crucial in emergency situations where there may not be enough time or equipment to test every patient's blood type.

Researchers are trying to solve this problem by turning other types of blood into something similar to type O. Then, what starts out as type A, AB, or B blood could safely be transfused into patients of any blood type. Blood type is determined by antigens on the surface of the RBCs. Each type of antigen is recognized and attacked by antibodies in other types of blood. Scientists are looking for chemicals that will clip the ends off the antigens so the recipient's antibodies won't recognize them as foreign. It's like making army recruits look more alike by giving all of them buzz cuts.

So far, this has worked fairly well with type B blood. Type B is uncommon, however. It would be much more useful to be able to convert type A blood. The A antigen is harder to remove, so it might take a few more years to figure out. The Rh-positive antigen is an even bigger puzzle. It has a complex structure that scientists don't yet fully understand. The conversion of Rh-positive blood to Rh-negative for transfusions is still far in the future.

Genetic Engineering

Someday, all plasma proteins used in component therapy might be made through genetic engineering. Albumin and antihemophilic factor are already being produced this way. To make albumin, for example, researchers isolate the gene for it—the instructions for how to make the protein—from human cells. They splice the gene into the genetic material of bacteria. Then the bacteria make albumin. Vats containing billions of bacteria churn out tons of albumin, which is then purified and used just like albumin from whole blood.

Since components made by genetic engineering don't come from donated blood, the supply of them doesn't depend on the number of donors. Best of all, the components don't carry viruses or other disease-causing germs.

Help with Hemoglobin

Plasma proteins can be injected into a patient, just as Lower infused substances into dogs' veins almost four hundred years ago. Hemoglobin requires a different approach. It's not dissolved in the plasma like albumin and other proteins are. Instead, it's inside RBCs. If the RBCs break open, their hemoglobin enters the blood and falls apart. The hemoglobin fragments damage blood vessels and kidneys. The same thing would happen if hemoglobin were injected into the bloodstream. But if we could inject hemoglobin, we could help millions of people who suffer from diseases such as sickle-cell anemia.

Doctors are trying several approaches. They're looking for ways to keep hemoglobin from falling apart when it's injected into the blood. Another approach is to make artificial RBCs to carry extra hemoglobin through the body. An artificial RBC is a bubble of fat, with hemoglobin inside it. By the time you read this, we may know whether these approaches work.

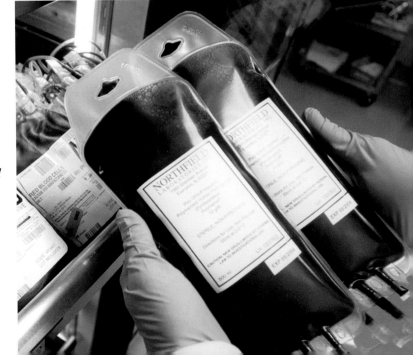

A technician holds two bags of PolyHeme, a blood substitute. PolyHeme contains hemoglobin removed from donated blood that is too old to be transfused into patients.

Better Testing

Protecting transfusion recipients from bloodborne diseases is a huge area of research. Doctors keep a sharp eye out for new diseases in the blood supply, develop tests for those new diseases, and work to improve the tests we already have.

Most of the tests now being used don't directly look for the microbes that cause disease. They look for antibodies that your body has made in response to the germs. They're good tests that prevent thousands of infections every year. But they also miss some, because the germs can be in your system for weeks before you make antibodies against them. If you donate blood after you have been infected but before you make those antibodies, your blood will test negative (healthy), yet it will carry the germ and be able to infect a transfusion recipient.

To identify an infection earlier, blood centers use a test called NAT. That stands for nucleic acid test. It detects the genetic material of infectious microbes. (It's similar to the way crime labs determine whether a hair or a drop of blood came from a specific suspect.) Using NAT, blood centers can now detect a hepatitis C infection just ten days after it starts. With the old antibody test, they couldn't detect the hepatitis virus until seventy to eighty days after the person became infected.

In 2004 scientists compared NAT with other tests for the AIDS and hepatitis C viruses. They found that NAT screening catches many infected donors that the older tests did not recognize—about five with HIV and fifty-six with hepatitis C every year. In other words, the old tests would have said blood from those sixty-one donors was safe to transfuse. Overall, NAT has lowered the risk of getting HIV or hepatitis C from a transfusion to one in two million.

One of the best things about NAT is that a test for a new disease can be developed quickly. In 2002 doctors identified several cases of West Nile virus that had been transmitted through a blood transfusion. West Nile virus, which normally spreads through mosquito bites, affects different people in different ways. Some who get West Nile aren't bothered at all. Others develop flu-like symptoms, and a few die. During an outbreak of West Nile virus in 2003, scientists put together an NAT screening within nine months—in time to identify and discard one thousand units of West Nile-infected blood. Many blood centers around the country now screen all their donations for West Nile virus.

Cleaning It Up

Even after careful testing, some infected blood slips through. Blood centers are working to find ways to kill or remove germs before the blood is transfused. They use heat to sterilize albumin. Other approaches include using detergents or ultraviolet light. The problem with these methods is that anything that kills bacteria or viruses often kills blood cells too. And chemicals used to treat a blood product might harm the recipient's cells when the treated blood product is transfused.

A different strategy is to remove the infectious agent, rather than killing it. For example, the cytomegalovirus lives inside leukocytes. If you remove those cells, you remove the virus too. Collection centers can pass blood through a special kind of filter that leukocytes stick to. This leukocyte reduction process yields RBCs and plasma proteins that are free of leukocytes and cytomegalovirus. Blood centers in Canada and many European countries use leukocyte reduction on all donated blood. In the United States, about 70 percent of donated blood goes through this process.

Bionic Blood

The ultimate in transfusion might be to do away with blood completely. Scientists are trying to develop a blood substitute that doesn't need to be refrigerated, can be stored for years before being used, won't carry any infectious diseases, can be given to recipients of any blood type, and will do all the jobs that real blood does.

One possibility is a group of chemicals called perfluorocarbons. They are liquids that can hold a lot of dissolved oxygen. In an amazing experiment done in 1966, mice survived for more than an hour submerged in liquid perfluorocarbon. They actually breathed through the fluid! Since then, researchers have tried injecting a perfluorocarbon into the bloodstream of a dog, cat, monkey, and human. It does carry oxygen through the system, but only for a short time. Then the patient needs to get a transfusion of whole blood or RBCs. Often the recipients suffer lung damage. But it's a promising start. Even if it only works for a few hours, a blood substitute could buy time in an emergency—enough time to get the patient to a hospital and a safe source of real blood.

Dog Donors—and Recipients

Dogs suffer many of the same blood diseases that afflict humans, including anemia and hemophilia. Now, nearly four hundred years after they helped Richard Lower launch the field of blood transfusion, dogs are beginning to benefit from the procedure themselves. So are cats, horses, cows, and llamas.

Veterinarians have done transfusions in dogs for many years. Until recently, they used blood from whatever dog was available to provide it. Without matching blood types, the transfusions often helped but sometimes hurt the recipient. Today, donor dog blood is typed. Dogs have about thirteen blood types, two of which can cause serious problems if the donor and recipient are not matched. The blood is also screened for diseases such as heartworm and Rocky Mountain spotted fever. As with humans, animals are rarely given whole blood. They receive RBCs, plasma, or platelets.

Some animal blood banks keep their donors in cages and tap them for a donation every few weeks. Others, such as the Eastern Veterinary Blood Bank in Annapolis, Maryland, recruit volunteer donors. Dog owners bring their pets in to donate several times a year. If an owner can't make it to the bank, the EVBB has two doggie bloodmobiles that go out into the community to gather donations.

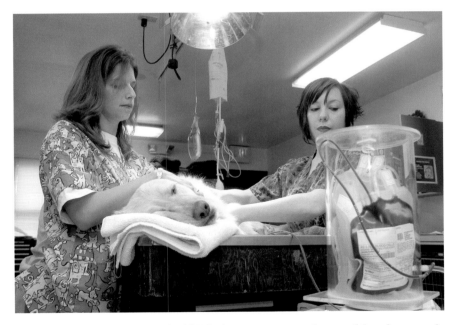

Dogs weighing 60 pounds (27 kg) or more can donate blood every six months.

The field of animal transfusion is a few decades behind transfusion work with humans. One obstacle is a shortage of donors. As more pet owners learn about animal blood banks and perhaps have a beloved pet receive a lifesaving transfusion, they may enlist their animals as donors.

Changing Ideas about Blood

In the introduction to this book we visited the bedside of a girl who was being bled to cure her fever and a modern emergency room where a crash victim was about to receive a transfusion. In the four centuries between those two scenes, ideas about blood have changed dramatically. We once tried to heal sickness by taking blood out of the patient. Then we did just the opposite, putting blood into the patient. We have learned how to turn blood into many different products and put into the patient only those that he needs. We're even beginning to make some of the products—or substitutes for them—without using blood at all.

Our ideas didn't change overnight. The word *breakthrough* sounds like something that happens quickly, but the key breakthroughs in blood transfusion took time. Sometimes scientists got stuck in one way of thinking, as when they relied on Galen's ancient wisdom. Sometimes scientists had new ideas but needed years of work to figure out how to apply them to patient care, as with Edwin Cohn's invention of component therapy.

Throughout the history of blood transfusion, scientists and doctors have not been the only ones whose ideas mattered. Everyone has a stake in the blood supply. Governments, blood banks, and companies have decided how to handle this most precious resource. Ordinary citizens such as sailors at Pearl Harbor and Ryan White have lived or died because of those decisions.

Blood is one of the most valuable gifts we can give other human beings and one of the most personal. Science has been able to copy some of the components of blood. It has not yet come up with a replacement for the real thing. Blood, in your body and mine, remains the fluid that gives life and health. The tainted-blood crisis of the 1980s reminds us that blood remains an almost magical substance that has the power to harm as well as the power to heal.

GLOSSARY

ABO group: one of the four major types of human blood (A, B, AB, and O)

acquired immunodeficiency syndrome (AIDS): the disease caused by the human immunodeficiency virus (HIV), which attacks and destroys some kinds of white blood cells

albumin: a protein in blood plasma that holds water in the blood vessels

anatomy: the structure and arrangement of parts of the body

anemia: a condition in which the body's tissues have too little oxygen. It results from having too few red blood cells or too little hemoglobin.

antibodies: proteins in the body that recognize and attack foreign material such as bacteria and viruses

anticoagulant: a chemical, such as sodium citrate, that prevents blood from clotting

antigen: a substance that doesn't belong in the body. Antibodies recognize antigens and destroy them.

arteries: blood vessels that carry blood away from the heart

bacteria: single-celled microorganisms that live in soil, water, air, plants, and animals. Some bacteria can cause disease.

blood pressure: the force blood exerts in the arteries as it is pumped through the body

blood type: *see* ABO group

capillaries: tiny blood vessels that connect arteries to veins

centrifuge: a device that spins liquid samples to separate them into their different components

circulatory system: the body system that moves blood throughout the body. It is made up of the heart and blood vessels.

citrate: an anticoagulant used to keep donated blood from clotting

clot: a wad of platelets, red blood cells, and plasma proteins that forms at the site of an injury to stop or slow the loss of blood

clotting cascade: a series of chemical reactions that results in the formation of a blood clot

clotting factors: proteins in blood plasma that control the formation of blood clots

component therapy: the use of individual substances from blood to treat specific ailments

cross-matching: testing whether a donor's blood matches a recipient's

fractionation: the separation of plasma into portions (fractions) that contain different proteins

fractions: groups of proteins that can be separated out of blood plasma

hemoglobin: a protein in red blood cells that carries oxygen and carbon dioxide

hemophilia: a hereditary disorder characterized by uncontrolled bleeding. It is caused by lack of a clotting factor.

hepatitis: one of several diseases that produce inflammation of the liver. The viruses that cause hepatitis B and hepatitis C can spread through transfusion of infected blood.

human immunodeficiency virus (HIV): the virus that causes AIDS

humors: the four bodily fluids that ancient people thought were responsible for a person's physical and mental health

leukemia: a disease in which the body makes too many white blood cells

leukocytes: white blood cells. Blood contains five kinds of leukocytes: neutrophils, basophils, lymphocytes, eosinophils, and monocytes.

phlebotomist: a person who is specially trained in the collection of blood

plasma: the liquid part of the blood

platelets: cell fragments that plug small holes in blood vessel walls and begin the clotting process

proteins: large, complex molecules that perform a wide variety of activities in cells

pulmonary loop: the part of the circulatory system that carries oxygen-poor blood from the heart to the lungs and oxygen-rich blood from the lungs back to the heart

red blood cells (RBCs): oxygen-carrying blood cells

Rh factor: a protein found on red blood cells of about 84 percent of people. These people are said to be Rh-positive.

serum: the liquid portion of blood (plasma) minus the clotting factors

shock: the body's reaction to a serious injury, characterized by very low blood pressure, loss of fluid from the blood vessels, rapid heartbeat, and possible organ failure

systemic loop: the part of the circulatory system that carries oxygen-rich blood from the heart throughout the body and returns oxygen-poor blood to the heart

transfusion: putting blood or blood products into a person

universal donor: a person with type O-negative blood, which can safely be transfused into anyone

universal recipient: a person with type AB-positive blood, who can receive any type of blood

valves: flaps of tissue in the heart and blood vessels that prevent blood from flowing in the wrong direction

veins: blood vessels that carry blood toward the heart

viruses: the smallest and simplest life-forms. Many diseases are caused by viruses.

SELECTED BIBLIOGRAPHY

Berkow, Robert, Mark H. Beers, and Andrew J. Fletcher, eds. *Merck Manual of Medical Information*. Home ed. Whitehouse Station, NJ: Merck Research Laboratories, 1997.

Christensen, Damaris. "Getting the Bugs Out of Blood." *Science News,* January 25, 2003, 59–61.

Colville, Thomas, and Joanna M. Bassert. *Clinical Anatomy and Physiology for Veterinary Technicians*. Saint Louis: Mosby, 2002.

Garrison, Fielding H. *An Introduction to the History of Medicine*. Philadelphia: W. B. Saunders, 1929.

Harmening, Denise M., ed. *Modern Blood Banking and Transfusion Practices*. 4th ed. Philadelphia: F. A. Davis, 1999.

Harvey, William. *On the Motion of the Heart and Blood in Animals*. Trans. Robert Willis. Buffalo: Prometheus Books, 1993.

Jardine, Lisa. *Ingenious Pursuits: Building the Scientific Revolution*. New York: Random House, 1999.

McCurnin, Dennis M., and Joanna M. Bassert. *Clinical Textbook for Veterinary Technicians*. 5th ed. Philadelphia: W. B. Saunders, 2002.

Moore, Pete. *Blood and Justice*. Chichester, UK: John Wiley, 2003.

Nuland, Sherwin B. *Doctors: The Biography of Medicine*. New York: Alfred A. Knopf, 1988.

Porter, Roy. *Blood and Guts: A Short History of Medicine*. New York: W. W. Norton, 2002.

Starr, Douglas. *Blood: An Epic History of Medicine and Commerce*. New York: HarperCollins, 2002.

Travis, John. "Blood Work." *Science News*, March 15, 2003, 171–172.

Wheater, P. R., H. G. Burkitt, and V. G. Daniels. *Functional Histology*. 2nd ed. New York: Churchill Livingstone, 1987.

FURTHER READING AND WEBSITES

BOOKS AND ARTICLES

DePrince, Elaine. *Cry Bloody Murder: A Tale of Tainted Blood*. New York: Random House, 1997.

Friedlander, Mark P., Jr. *Outbreak: Disease Detectives at Work*. Minneapolis: Twenty-First Century Books, 2003.

Moore, Pete. *Blood and Justice: The Seventeenth-Century Parisian Doctor Who Made Blood Transfusion History*. Hoboken, NJ: Wiley, 2003.

Starr, Douglas. *Blood: An Epic History of Medicine and Commerce*. New York: HarperCollins, 2002.

Storad, Conrad J. *Inside AIDS: HIV Attacks the Immune System*. Minneapolis: Twenty-First Century Books, 1998.

Trice, Linda. *Charles Drew: Pioneer of Blood Plasma*. New York: McGraw-Hill, 2000.

Walker, Richard. *DK Guide to the Human Body*. New York: Dorling Kindersley, 2001.

White, Ryan, and Ann Marie Cunningham. *Ryan White: My Own Story*. New York: Dial Books, 1991.

Yount, Lisa. *William Harvey: Discoverer of How Blood Circulates*. Berkeley Heights, NJ: Enslow Publishers, 1994.

WEBSITES

Centers for Disease Control and Prevention
http://www.cdc.gov
   The CDC website has lots of information on bloodborne diseases.

Eastern Veterinary Blood Bank
http://www.evbb.com
   This site describes the history of animal transfusion and tells how to enlist your pet as a donor.

History of Blood Transfusion
http://members.rediff.com/bloodbank/History.htm
   This site offers a timeline of transfusion history.

International Federation of Red Cross and Red Crescent Societies
http://www.ifrc.org
This website carries updates on the need for blood in disaster and war zones throughout the world.

Mayo Clinic
http://www.mayoclinic.org
At this site, you can find easy-to-read information about blood types, transfusions, and bloodborne diseases.

National Hemophilia Foundation
http://www.hemophilia.org
This website offers information and help to people with hemophilia, as well as their families, friends, and doctors.

Red Gold: The Epic Story of Blood
http://www.pbs.org/wnet/redgold/
This website, based on the PBS program *Red Gold*, features biographies of blood pioneers, basics of blood biology, and highlights from the history of transfusion.

INDEX

acquired immunodeficiency
syndrome (AIDS), 24,
73–74, 75, 76, 78, 79,
80, 81, 84, 98
American Red Cross, 60,
65, 71–72; and blood
drives, 65–66, 71
anemia, 22, 49, 73, 84,
100; hemolytic disease
of the newborn, 49, 73;
sickle-cell, 22, 77
antibodies, 23, 27, 45,
47–48, 49, 59, 64, 92,
96, 98
anticoagulants, 50–51, 86
antigens, 45, 47–49, 96
arteries, 14, 16, 17, 18, 19,
31, 34, 36, 37, 54, 55

bacteria. *See* microbes
Bethune, Norman, 53–54
bleeding, 7, 8, 9, 10, 15,
102; common medical
treatment, 9, 11–13, 14,
19; cupping, 11–12; and
death, 13; leeches, 12,
93; modern-day, 93–94
blood, 7, 8, 10, 11, 27;
cleaning, 99; collection or
donation of, 57, 60,
66–67, 71, 75, 76, 79,
80, 90; components of,
27, 65, 68, 69, 89;
demand for, 50, 51, 57,
65–67, 90; discoveries in,
18–19; early beliefs about,
9, 13, 14, 27, 32, 69;
essence of a person in, 13,
33–34, 37–38; flow of,
16, 17, 18–19; function
of, 21; loss of, 10;
processing of, 87–89; and
race, 71–72; reaction to

foreign, 35, 37–38; and
screening, 77, 79, 80;
storage of, 43, 52–54, 57,
68, 81, 89; substitute,
100; testing for disease,
88–89, 98–99; typing,
87–88. *See also* bleeding
blood products; plasma;
platelets; red blood cells
(RBCs); white blood cells
(WBCs)
blood banks, 8, 53, 55, 71,
74, 76, 77, 80, 81, 89,
94, 95, 102; animal,
101–102
blood donation, 83–89, 90;
autologous, 92; and
bloodborne disease, 84,
98; dog, 100–102;
interview during, 84–85;
procedure, 85–87; and
tattoos or piercings, 84,
85. *See also* phlebotomists
blood products, 8, 59, 65,
66, 77, 78, 79, 80, 99
blood supply, 50, 102; safety
of, 77, 79–80, 81, 98–99
blood type, 22, 27, 39, 43,
44–49, 51, 52, 91; A, 22,
45, 47–48, 87, 88, 95,
96; AB, 22, 45, 46,
47–49, 88, 90, 95; B, 22,
45, 47–49, 87, 88, 90,
95, 96; and inheritance,
47–48, 49; manipulating,
95–96; matching, 43, 46,
57, 91–92, 95; O, 22,
45, 46, 47–49, 54, 55,
88, 90, 95; Rh factor,
48–49, 95, 96
Blundell, James, 38–39, 43

capillaries, 17, 18, 19, 21,

22, 45
Cesalpino, Andrea, 18, 19,
29
circulation, 29;
experimentation of,
29–30
circulatory system, 17, 18,
19
clots, 21, 24, 26, 37, 77,
94. *See also* clotting
cascade; clotting factors;
hemophilia; platelets
(thrombocytes)
clotting, 43, 53–51, 64,
67. *See also*
anticoagulants
clotting cascade, 24–25,
26–27
clotting factors, 25, 26, 27,
65, 68, 77
Coga, Arthur, 35–36
Cohn, Edwin, 62–63, 64,
65–66, 71, 102
component therapy, 65,
68–69, 96, 102

Denis, Jean-Baptiste,
33–34, 35–38, 40, 83;
arrest of, 38
dogs, 100; experiments with,
18, 29–32, 33, 50, 97
Drew, Charles, 59–61, 71, 72

erythrocytes. *See* red blood
cells (RBCs)

Galen, 13–15, 16, 18, 102
germs. *See* microbes
Greeks, ancient, medical
beliefs of, 9, 10, 13

Harvey, William, 18–19,
27, 29

ABOUT THE AUTHOR

Cherie Winner is a science writer for *Washington State Magazine*. She also writes books. Her published titles include *Cryobiology, Life in the Tundra, Life on the Edge, Salamanders, Trout,* and *Woodpeckers.* Winner holds a Ph.D. in zoology from Ohio State University.

PHOTO ACKNOWLEDGMENTS

The images in this book are used with the permission of: © Dr. Dennis Kunkel/Visuals Unlimited, pp. 1, 20; PhotoDisc Royalty Free by Getty Images, pp. 2, all backgrounds; © Abeles/Photo Researchers, Inc., p. 6; © Bettmann/CORBIS, pp. 9, 40, 62; © British Library/HIP/Art Resource, NY, p. 10; © The Art Archive/University Library Prague/ Dagli Orti, p. 12; © Hulton Archive/Getty Images, p. 14; © The Art Archive/Private Collection Italy/Dagli Orti, p. 16; © Laura Westlund/Independent Picture Service, p. 17; © Dr. Stanley Flegler/Visuals Unlimited, p. 22; © Dr. David Phillips/Visuals Unlimited, p. 23; © Dr. Robert Caughey/Visuals Unlimited, p. 25; © Martin M. Rotker/Photo Researchers, Inc., p. 26; © The Royal Society, p. 28; © Science Photo Library/Photo Researchers, Inc., p. 36; Print Collection, Miriam and Ira D. Wallach Division of Art, Prints and Photographs, The New York Public Library, Astor, Lenox and Tilden Foundations, p. 39; Courtesy The National Library of Medicine, p. 41; © Keystone/Hulton Archive/ Getty Images, pp. 44, 66; The Mount Sinai Archives, p. 46; AP Images, pp. 54, 70; © Hampton/Hulton Archive/Getty Images, p. 56; © The Art Archive/National Archives, p. 58; © Alfred Eisenstaedt/Time & Life Pictures/Getty Images, p. 61; AP Images/U.S. Signal Corps, p. 67; AP Images/Gene J. Puskar, p. 73; © David Scharf/Science Faction/ Getty Images, p. 75 (left); © George Musil/Visuals Unlimited, p. 75 (right); © Kim Komenich/Time & Life Pictures/Getty Images, p. 78; © Michael Donne/Photo Researchers, p. 82; © Alan Powdrill/Taxi/Getty Images, p. 85; © Antonia Reeve/Photo Researchers, Inc., pp. 86, 89; © Will & Deni McIntyre/Photo Researchers, Inc., p. 88; © Kim Komenich/San Francisco Chronicle/CORBIS, p. 90; © Jim Varney/Photo Researchers, Inc., p. 91; © Alex Bartel/ Photo Researchers, Inc., p. 92; © Lester Lefkowitz/CORBIS, p. 94; AP Images/M. Spencer Green, p. 97; AP Images/Newport News-Daily Press, Brett England, p. 101.

Front cover: © Tom Schierlitz/Stone/Getty Images.
Back cover: PhotoDisc Royalty Free by Getty Images.